THE LOGIC OF
BUSINESS STRATEGY

An Abt Books/Ballinger Publication

THE LOGIC OF
BUSINESS STRATEGY

BRUCE HENDERSON

BALLINGER PUBLISHING COMPANY
Cambridge, Massachusetts
A Subsidiary of Harper & Row, Publishers, Inc.

200832

International Standard Book Number: 0-88410-983-6

Library of Congress Catalog Card Number: 84-11119

Printed in the United States of America

Library of Congress Cataloging in Publication Data

Henderson, Bruce D.

    The logic of business strategy.

    Includes bibliographical references and index.
    1. Corporate planning. I. Title.
HD30.28H47   658.4'012   84-11119
ISBN 0-88410-983-6

CONTENTS

LIST OF FIGURES AND TABLES

FIGURES

TABLES

1 STRATEGIC CONCEPTS

1. THE CONCEPT OF STRATEGY

The Beginning of Natural Competition

Competition existed long before strategy: It began with life itself. The first one-cell organisms required certain resources for maintenance of life. When those resources were adequate, each generation became greater in number than the preceding one. If there had been no limitation on required resources, exponential growth would have led to infinite numbers. But as life evolved, single-cell life became a food resource for more complex life; with greater complexity, each level became the resource for the next higher level. When two competitors were in perpetual competition, one inevitably displaced the other, unless something prevented it. In the absence of some counterbalancing force that maintained a stable equilibrium between two competitors by giving each an advantage in his own territory, only one survived.

Over millions of years, a complex web of competitive interaction developed. Today, more than a million distinct species have been catalogued. Each has a unique advantage in competition for its required resources within its particular niche of the environment. There are believed to be millions more such variations of species as yet unclassified.

Since each of these competitors must be unique, the abundance of variations must match an equal variation in potential factors which define a niche and the

1

varied characteristics in the environment which make that combination effective. The richer the environment, the more severe the competition and the greater the number of competitors. Likewise, the richer the environment, the smaller the differences among competitors.

This is consistent with biological research of the recent past. Experimental laboratory ecologists discovered in the 1930s and 1940s that if two similar species of small organisms are put together in a bottle with food and uniform substrate, only one species can persist.[1] The observation that coexisting species in nature do differ ecologically and that species must differ ecologically to coexist in bottles led to Gause's Competitive Exclusion Principle: "No two species can coexist who make their living in the same way."

For millions of years natural competition involved no strategy. It was natural selection: adaptation and survival of the fittest. Random chance determined the mutations and variations that survived and succeeded to compound their numbers. Those who left relatively fewer offspring became displaced. Those who adapted best displaced the rest. Physical and structural characteristics adapted, but behavior adapted also and became embedded in instinctual reactions.

The awareness of natural competition as a systematic effect is centuries old. Malthus quoted Benjamin Franklin's observation about the crowding out of natural competition. Darwin himself credited Malthus with the insight. Wallace and Darwin, separated by thousands of miles, simultaneously developed the concept of natural selection by competition. Darwin emphasized repeatedly the overriding importance of competition: It is awesome in its potential for evolution.

As far as we know, only primates possess imagination and the ability to reason logically. But without these capabilities, behavior and tactics are either intuitive or the result of conditioned reflexes. Strategy is impossible. Strategy depends upon the ability to foresee the future consequences of present initiatives.

The Beginning of Strategic Competition

Strategy in its most elementary form most likely developed when the hunting party was formed by early humans to capture large game that could not have been handled by a single individual. But this was hardly true strategy. The quarry itself could have no counter strategy, only its instinctive behavior. True strategy was probably first practiced by one tribe attempting to take over the hunting grounds of another tribe.

For strategy to be possible, it is necessary to be able to imagine and evaluate the possible consequences of alternate courses of action. But imagination and reasoning power are not sufficient. There also must be knowledge of competition and the characteristic higher order effects of alternative actions. That knowledge must reach a critical mass before it becomes significant. Until enough relationships have been integrated to see the whole pattern, knowledge is no more than the individual pieces of a jigsaw puzzle.

The basic requirements for strategy development are:

- a critical mass of knowledge;
- ability to integrate all of this knowledge and examine it as an interactive dynamic system;
- skill at system analysis sufficient to understand sensitivity, time lags, immediate and future possibilities and consequences;
- imagination and logic to choose between specific alternatives;
- resource control beyond immediate needs; and
- the will to forego current benefits in order to invest in the future potential.

Simple as these requirements may seem, they are absent in natural competition. Strategic competition requires an ability to understand the dynamics of the complex web of natural competition. The value of strategy in competition comes from developing the potential to intervene in a complex system with only a limited input and thereby produce a predictable and desired change in the system's equilibrium.

Strategy, as a concept, probably emerged in connection with military operations. All of the elements were present that made strategy valuable:

- finite resources;
- uncertainty about an adversary's capability and intentions;
- irreversible commitment of resources;
- necessity of coordinating action over time and distance;
- uncertainty about control of the initiative; and
- the critical nature of the adversaries' mutual perceptions of each other.

History books tend to tell us the sequence of events and who won a war. They tell us less about why the initiator thought it was worth taking the risk and even less about the strategy of each adversary. Strategy is often not clear or obvious even with the benefit of hindsight. Sun Tsu, a general in 500 B.C., said it well: "All men can see the tactics whereby I conquer, but what none can see is the strategy out of which victory is evolved." The history of strategy is rarely more than rationalization.

There are many analogies between business and military strategy. One in particular is quite important: Visible conflict is only a periodic symptom of a continuing effort to manage a dynamic equilibrium between adversaries.

Visible hot wars are the result of instability in the competitive relationship. This instability is subtle and complex; it is not easily seen or understood. There are two basic reasons for this instability. First, no one logically starts a war in which the inevitable destruction to both adversaries is more than offset by the combination of favorable odds and potential positive net payoffs. Second, many of the events that lead to a progressive destabilization of equilibrium are emotional and not necessarily logical. The aggression which is inherent in warfare is unavoidably destructive, but the outcome may seem to be potentially valuable enough to at least one party to justify the initiative.

The relationships of geopolitical strategy are more comparable to business strategy than the battles that usually mark the turning points in military conflict. The ultimate objective for both participants is stability with peace and greater prosperity on a sustainable basis.

The Underlying Principles and Objectives of Strategy

Many of the basic principles of strategy have been distilled from warfare. Liddell Hart, the military historian, stated and collected some basic principles:

> The true aim is not so much to seek battle as to seek a strategic situation so advantageous that if it does not of itself produce the decision, its continuation by a battle is sure to achieve this.

> But we can at least crystallize the lessons into two simple maxims—one negative, the other positive. The first is that, in face of the overwhelming evidence of history, no general is justified in launching his troops to a direct attack upon an enemy firmly in position. The second, that instead of seeking to upset the enemy's equilibrium by one's attack, it must be upset before a real attack is, or can be successfully launched.

> The principles of war, not merely one principle, can be condensed into a single word—"concentration." But for truth this needs to be amplified as the "concentration of strength against weakness."

> —Hart

The whole art of war consists in a well reasoned and extremely circumspect defensive, followed by a rapid and audacious attack.

—Napoleon

Supreme excellence consists in breaking the enemy's resistance without fighting. Thus the highest form of generalship is to baulk the enemy's plans; the next best is to prevent the junction of the enemy's forces; the next in order is to attack the enemy's army in the field; the worst policy of all is to besiege walled cities.

In all fighting, the direct method may be used for joining battle, but indirect methods will be needed in order to secure victory.

—Sun Tsu

The most complete and happy victory is this: to compel one's enemy to give up his purpose, while suffering no harm oneself.

—Belisarius[1]

The underlying concepts of strategy involve the allocation and concentration of resources, the need for communication and mobility, the element of surprise, and the advantage of the defense. However, military strategy concepts revolve around the assumption that open battle has already begun. Hart introduced the concept of "grand strategy"—the plan for securing and stabilizing the peace for which the war is fought. This is an aspect of strategy that is of the greatest importance to business. Business strategy must manage a constantly shifting dynamic equilibrium with multiple competitors.

For business, as for nations, continued coexistence is the ultimate objective, not the elimination of the competitor. The purpose of the strategy in both peace and war is a future stable relationship with respect to the competitors on the most favorable possible terms and conditions.

The emergence of grand strategy concepts for business has been severely handicapped by the lack of a comprehensive general theory of dynamic competition. Only in game theory has a systematic and methodical approach been developed. But a general theory of competition now appears possible and imminent.

The Beginning of a General Theory of Competition

There has always been conflict and competition for scarce resources. Strategy has been practiced whenever an advantage was gained by planning the sequence and timing of the deployment of resources while simultaneously taking into account the probable capabilities and behavior of competition. But insight into this experience has rarely been integrated conceptually as a competitive system. Many aspects of competition were explored in great depth but rarely as a dynamic system in equilibrium.

The natural field of study that should have been expected to generate such insight was economics. For whatever reason, philosophical constraints on assumptions and their implications were biased, and economics earned the name of the "dismal science." It remained for a most unlikely discipline, biology, to develop the foundation of a general theory of competition. However, this emerged after considerable progress had already been made in the field of business strategy development.

Trials and Errors of Conceptual Development

The history of the general public's conceptual insight into the U.S. economic system can, to some extent, be judged by the evolution of the antitrust laws and the implicit assumptions embedded in them. The antitrust laws were precipitated at the turn of the century by the efforts of Standard Oil to integrate. Its tactics were to concentrate on a local competitor and undersell until it capitulated. In the absence of competition, Standard Oil could thereafter charge higher prices to recoup its losses. As strategy, it was excellent short term. As grand strategy, it was flawed. It caused very damaging second-order effects.

Since the turn of the century, antitrust laws have been interpreted and reinterpreted by the courts in the light of past and then-current concepts of competition. The evolution of theory represented the gradual development of generally accepted models of competitive behavior. Unfortunately, these competitive models were highly theoretical and simplistic. They were also based on untested and dogmatic assumptions. Semantics played an important role. "Perfect competition" became a goal. "Perfect competition" was meant to describe an idealized situation in which all competitors were so small that no one individual competitor could have any perceptible effect on supply or demand and therefore on price. No situation of this kind has ever existed except for very short periods. Such a situation is inherently unstable. But all alternate models were labeled "imperfect competition."

The conceptual model developed through court interpretation was quite simplistic. Although scale effects and their inherent instability were recognized, they were brushed aside. A never-tested assumption that optimum scale is only a fraction of industry size was necessary for the presumption that multiple competitors are in stable equilibrium. The assumption that all cost-versus-scale curves are L-shaped or U-shaped was also a fundamental premise for competitive equilibrium to exist without monopoly. Assumptions were made that within a generalized industry all competition is essentially head to head.

These assumptions were further compounded by confusion as to whether the objective was to protect competitors from each other or to protect competition as a concept. And, of course, all of the assumptions were made within the constraints imposed by legal concepts of property and social organization.

Such constraints were simplistic enough to sharply distort a realistic view of the nature of competition. As a consequence, substantial inhibitions were created in the business community toward the usage of certain words and phrases like "dominate," "preempt share," "capture market," "match price," and so forth.

In and of itself this was minor compared to the inhibitions created with respect to the thinking about competitive interaction between specific pairs of competitors. Yet the interaction between specific pairs of competitors who vie for specific needed and scarce resources is the essence of strategy.

This is a generic problem inherent in any strategy. Characteristically, for any competitor there are many such pairs of competitors to be dealt with simultaneously. The realities of competition forced businessmen, often as a matter of course, to think in such terms. But the effect was to suppress open discussion and conceptual development of business strategy except in a peripheral way.

The Emergence of Explicit Business Strategy

Strategy, by its very nature, is like a poker game and not subject to accurate reconstruction by either kibitzers or historians. However, there are a few classic examples such as the General Motors segmentation strategy developed by Alfred P. Sloan against Ford's Model T. But this occurred in the early 1930s. Soon the focus was centered on war efforts. To a considerable extent, the emergence of concepts of business strategy can be traced to the late 1950s and the early 1960s.

Several streams of thought converged to produce the focus on business strategy that blossomed in the 1970s. These included:

- the problems of strategy development within a complex organization;
- the problems of strategy execution within a complex organization;

- the problems of information in a complex organization; and
- the problems of control in a multiple business organization sharing common resources.

Many of these were foreshadowed by the development of the giant organizations and trusts of the early twentieth century, which precipitated the antitrust laws. In the United States many of these were monolithic, single-industry, narrow-range product organizations. Conspicuous examples were the oil and steel companies, with the automobile companies close behind. Characteristically, scale was a critical factor.

However, simultaneously, the multiproduct companies were beginning to emerge. The electric manufacturing companies that had their birth in the latter part of the nineteenth century were inherently multiproduct.

Although examples of large multiproduct companies had emerged in Europe even earlier, the European environment was different from the American environment. Consequently, the multiproduct companies in Europe had different characteristics.

When small countries are constrained by trade barriers at their boundaries, then the trade market area is inherently small. Large scale could come only from multiple product companies in small countries. Banks and banking institutions constituted the only source of capital for most concerns. Frequently such financial institutions were large equity owners. In such countries, the interaction between the financial institutions and with the government tended to inhibit freewheeling competition. In such small markets, specialization produced very small scale. The generalist had an advantage. Short distances prevented the growth of regional competitors who were isolated initially but who with increasing infrastructure and transportation capability later became competitors in other regions.

In the early twentieth century, when Japan abandoned its policy of self-imposed isolation, the same pattern emerged. However, in the United States a quite different pattern developed that instead of inhibiting competitive strategy required it.

A vast and growing market without barriers or regulation except logistics favored the generalist initially but forced specialization as the market density increased. A large and dense market offers economies of scale to the specialist. But increased specialization on a national scale also means increased competition with finer and finer subdivisions of the market into competitive segments. The ability to define those competitive segments, determine who sets the boundaries, appraise the potential within those boundaries, and assess the opportunity for redefinition of boundaries becomes ever more valuable. The need for strategy increased even though the understanding of it did not.

Unlike those in Europe and Japan, U.S. banking institutions were often unstable and highly fragmented until well into the twentieth century. This removed a major influence from the development of competitive growth patterns and imposed much of the responsibility for financing growth or success back upon the earnings retained in the business. The absence of an income tax on corporate earnings greatly increased the degree of competition and the need for internal financial resources. In some measure, this laid the foundation for multiproduct companies such as Westinghouse and General Electric, which in turn presaged the conglomerates that developed following World War II.

In all strategy the ultimate objectives tend to be access to and control of the required resources. For business this almost always includes money, supplies, markets, and recruits. Money, or its equivalent, comes first. This may have been the underlying cause of the development of the multiproduct or conglomerate form of company.

The multiproduct form of organization is particularly well suited for continual growth of a business organization in the same way that a multigeneration family pattern is well suited to propagation of the species over time. The impact of this is almost entirely in capital formation and reallocation rather than in marketing, manufacturing, or technology. Those business areas that succeed and reach full potential are characteristically unable to reinvest in themselves at rates equal to their capital generation. Conversely, they are well positioned to finance the young, rapidly growing segments of their company, which offer investment potential far in excess of any possible capital self-generation.

An additional area of potential for the multiproduct company was sharing of experience and scale across related but not identical products and services even though the competitive segments served by the products were different. This too was greatly facilitated by the absence of any income tax complications on the internal expense financing as well as the lack of the inherent overhead in external financing and other supply interfaces.

From Strategy to Structure

All of these factors made the United States a seedbed for productivity increase. But this very dynamism and complexity increased the importance of a conceptual framework for strategy development rather than an intuitive base for resource deployment and management. Tactics can be learned from experience, but strategy cannot. Strategy is nonobvious management of a system over time. Good strategy must be based primarily on logic, not primarily on experience derived from intuition.

Perhaps the greatest insight into the complexity of the management of the large corporation was provided by Chester Barnard in his book, *The Functions of the Executive*. Chandler and Salsbury later provided additional insight into the relationships between strategy and structure in *Pierre S. DuPont and the Making of the Modern Corporation*. Alfred P. Sloan also revealed some of his strategy concerns in *My Years with General Motors*.

The foundation of Sloan's success with General Motors' management was divisional autonomy with central control combined with the separation of policy and operations. However, the emergence of structural and organizational problems and their connection with strategy were foreshadowed prior to World War II.

Both Westinghouse and General Electric changed from functional control by central management to profit center management prior to World War II. But it was not until the early 1950s when General Electric, under Ralph Cordiner, carried the profit center concept to extremes, and General Electric became identified publicly as the pioneer and leader of this structural architecture, which rapidly became widespread.

However, profit center organization soon began to reveal some problems. Carried to one extreme, there was no function for central management except as an interface with the banks and tax collector. At the opposite extreme, the profit center was only a symbol. The proliferation of corporate staff and the leverage of its influence effectively wiped out the independent profit center as a functioning unit. The parallel between the king and his troubles with the barons suggests the problem is not a new one.

The Dilemma of Decentralized Strategy

In large-scale, diversified, multiproduct companies it was impractical for central management to be familiar in depth with each business, each product, each competitive segment, and each unit's implied strategy. This led to more and more reliance on short-term financial control measures. This in turn rapidly led toward more short-term suboptimization of results.

The inevitable short-range viewpoint induced by quarterly profit measurements as the prime control often confined profit center management to tactical resource management only. In such a context, there also was little real management judgment possible at the corporate level with respect to overall strategy except with regard to financial policy. This conflict between strategy and structure may account for a company such as Westinghouse having been a pioneer and technical leader in products that ranged from automobile generators to television tubes to silicon transistors and integrated circuits yet enjoying no success in these products. On the other hand, when the developments were clearly strategic enough to threaten the core business of the company, Westinghouse became a world leader in such developments as alternating current machinery and later atomic power.

By the late 1950s it was becoming obvious that something more than profit centers or profit centers with large corporate functional staffs were needed. The corporate staffs tended to regard themselves as the real source of policy and direction in much the same way that government agencies do. In the same fashion, large corporate staff represented a heavy drain on the time, energy, and initiative of operating unit management.

Later this dilemma was to encourage the development of long-range planning and then strategy development. Before that period, however, the "five-year plan" became the centerpiece of performance measurement and control. The use of such a forecast became widespread.

Although five-year plans provided a basis for discussion, they were almost a charade. The budgetary process and the five-year plan became almost inseparable. In the absence of an integrated, coherent strategy based on system analysis and coordinated planning, it was inevitable that five-year plans could be no more than forecasts that were then frozen into budgets.

The characteristic five-year plan promised results that were based on a somewhat higher price realization forecast, a somewhat higher market share forecast, and a somewhat lower cost forecast. They were revised annually to reduce the forecasted performance overall, yet to maintain a trend-line forecast of ever higher achievement.

Such a pattern was inevitable in the absence of a fundamental strategy as the basis of the plan. There is no reason to expect a change in competitive equilibrium in the absence of a plan to cause it to happen. Incremental improvement in costs can be expected on the basis of the experience curve phenomenon. Most companies have long records of such reductions. So do their competitors. How can an improvement in long-term performance be forecast in the absence of a prediction of a *differential* change in competitive capability?

Five-year plans evolved into hoped-for goals rather than significant shifts in competitive relationships. This was the common situation when the concept of long-range planning first emerged.

In spite of the research into business administration and all functional aspects of business, the exploration of competitive situations by consulting firms, and a few books on the planning process such as those by Steiner, there were no organized efforts to explore and develop an approach to the subject until Stanford Research Institute developed the Long Range Planning Service in the early 1960s. The SRI Long Range Planning Service was in no sense a strategy approach for a given company, nor was Arthur D. Little's Service to Investors, which was quite similar. In both cases the firms drew on their breadth of knowledge of technical process to evaluate the development of the market itself. To do this well required some assessment of the competitive system as a whole and its behavior for specific sectors.

At about the same time, the word "development" came into common usage. The corporate staff position of director of corporate development began to appear in announcements in the press. The duties and responsibilities of such positions were highly variable. Apparently they were to evaluate the position and direction of the company as a whole in order to develop alternatives that promised to lead to more desirable outcomes.

Another corporate title, director of planning, soon appeared. Then in some companies the title director of strategic planning emerged. This somewhat ambiguous and redundant title served a purpose. It was an indication of a gradually shifting focus toward strategy as a concept. Although the role itself has never been clear, the value of staff work in preparation for strategy development achieved increased recognition.

The Approach to a Critical Mass of Knowledge

By the mid-1960s, many of the pieces needed for the development of business strategy were in place. Although Morgenstern and von Neumann's studies of game theory[2] were directly applicable when published in 1953 and Jay Forrester's 1961 studies of the feedback loops and higher-order effects of dynamic systems[3] offered substantial insights into the possibility of quantitative modeling of competitive interaction, these studies were somewhat before their time in terms of being integrated with other concepts. There was still nothing resembling a general theory of competition. Acceptance of the "perfect competition" theory of microeconomics was still high.

In the mid-1960s observations by The Boston Consulting Group brought into question some of the underlying assumptions of "perfect competition." BCG made the first presentation to a client of projections and recommendations based on the experience curve effect in 1966[4]. During the next fifteen years this characteristic cost behavior pattern became conventional wisdom in business in most of the developed countries. Even government regulators, whose policies had been based on incompatible assumptions, conceded its validity but continued to argue about its eventual application.[5]

The experience curve theory postulated that in complex products and services, costs corrected for inflation typically decline about 20 to 30 percent each time total accumulated experience doubles. This was a statement of pragmatic observations easily observable and testable. The simplicity of the statement, however, did not reveal the complexity of the interaction or, if this were typical, the far-reaching implications.

The learning curve had first been observed in the 1920s. During World War II it had been observed repeatedly in the labor hours required for building aircraft. However, the characteristic cost declines from learning applied to labor hours were far less than the observed cost declines in the total cost as expressed in the experience curve.

Some reflection makes it obvious that all cost components do not go down in cost at equal rates. This means they follow different cost decline rates. They share different amounts of experience with other uses. The end products for different uses have differing elasticities. Substitution of cost elements is not only possible, it is also inevitable. That is probably why the experience curve is so much steeper in its cost decline than the learning curve. There were many years between the recognition of the learning curve phenomenon and the far-reaching implications of the same pattern with respect to overall cost as seen in the experience curve.

All costs and cost effects, except inflation, are included in the experience curve. This includes cost of capital and scale effects. Ordinarily these effects are obscured by accounting conventions that try to match expenditures with revenue over long time spans. The experience curve is an exponential smoothing of the ratio of cash flow to output. Conventional accounting treatment of experience-related costs (such as research and development, advertising, staff development, etc.) is impossible to couple with cash flow because of the uncertainty of the effect both on timing and in the amount of output that eventually leads to revenue. All accounting is consequently either a forecast or a smoothing model. The experience curve, however, is the rate of change in cash flow expenditures plotted against accumulated units of output. In this form it too is an exponentially smoothed curve.

The significant facts have far-reaching implications:

- The experience curve costs are a reasonably accurate approximation of cash flow versus volume.
- These curves apparently never turn upward in cost.
- Market share soon becomes a direct surrogate for experience.
- If the growth rate is constant, so is the rate of cost decline.
- Individual competitors tend to follow parallel, but not congruent, cost slopes if their market shares remain stable.

The experience curve is only a schematic pattern for normative behavior. But if the experience curve is representative, then the stability of competitive relationships postulated in the concept of "perfect competition" could never exist; nor could the basic assumption of conventional microeconomic theory— that all cost-versus-volume curves are L- or U-shaped and turn up far below available market volume.

The strong and long-held convictions about "perfect competition" and "cost curve shape" had a reason. Without those assumptions, competitive stability was improbable under any circumstances. The whole foundation for public policy and conventional strategy analysis would have disappeared otherwise.

Nothing can take the place of such theory without acceptance of the idea that every competitor is uniquely superior and dominates his competitive segment as a virtual monopolist. Later insights from other sources were to demonstrate that this was probably literally true. But acceptance of such radical notions takes time. It was a dozen years before understandable and acceptable alternatives for business use came into the open.

There is, or should be, a direct functional relationship between market share and cost that is in effect a relationship between cash generation and market share.

- A business requires cash to invest in its assets as it grows.
- A rapidly growing business will require very large amounts of investment, usually more than it can finance from retained earnings.
- A slowly growing successful business cannot continually reinvest in itself faster than it grows.

The simple implication is that a corporation is a portfolio of businesses, each of which has differing cash needs and differing cash generation capabilities. But the corporation as a whole must be consistently within certain bounds in its cash flows.

The growth/share matrix developed by The Boston Consulting Group led to colloquial expressions for differing combinations, such as "star," "cash cow," "question mark," and "dog," which became part of the business vocabulary.

Several other consulting firms developed their own versions of the relevant tradeoffs and combinations. The best known was McKinsey's tradeoff of industry attractiveness versus the company's own competitive strength. This more generalized matrix accurately reflected the large number of variables that needed to be integrated into a realistic analysis. However, it gave no indication of or guidance on the relationships or how they integrated but merely pointing out the implications of certain combinations of appraisals.

The Boston Consulting Group model was based on a far more logical and quantitative set of relationships. But it too was dependent upon accuracy and precision in defining relevant markets and evaluation of market shares.

Neither of these displays was really useful except as a guide to a logical way of thinking about competitive relationships. But they were a step toward the concept of a model of competition as an interactive dynamic system.

All of these hypotheses and constructs were the subject of considerable discussion that eventually included the academic community and particularly the leading graduate schools of business. While these ideas were still controversial, they were included in case materials and class discussions and argued in academic journals. Harvard Business School meanwhile became deeply involved in a project that had originated at General Electric under Dr. Sidney Schoeffler. Professor Robert Buzzell and Dr. Schoeffler succeeded in using computerized data from multiple sources to correlate the relationship between various factors and profitability. The system became widely known as PIMS, an acronym for Profit Impact of Market Strategy. The PIMS program provided many interesting insights and the basis for a number of hypotheses. One in particular was quite timely. The correlation between market share and profitability was demonstrated beyond any reasonable doubt.

Yet even in the late 1970s no general theory of competition had been developed. There was no integrating concept.

The Integration of Strategic Knowledge

There was not even a credible hypothesis to replace the suspect reference provided by traditional concepts of "perfect competition." However, a potentially revolutionary conceptual insight was about to become the subject of general discussion. Its source was a most unexpected one: biology and more specifically sociobiology.

In retrospect, a number of books had been published during the preceding period that cast a great deal of light on the potential of a general theory of strategy and competition. Some of these, such as Antony Jay's *Management and Machiavelli*, Robert Ardrey's *African Genesis*, and Desmond Morris' *The Naked Ape*, seemed more like popular bestsellers than the cutting edge of the state of the art.

However, some were relevant to the hypothesis of the emerging disciples of ethology, a brand of biology. The significance of this inquiry was emphasized when Konrad Lorenz, author of *On Aggression* and of *Studies in Animal and Human Behavior*, received a Nobel prize. His fellow Nobel laureate, Tinbergen, was working in the same field. Their writing and research, as well as the more popularized versions of Ardrey and Morris, were concerned with aspects of evolution and behavior. Inevitably all of this tended to include a large component of competitive behavior.

In 1975, after the expiration of the required thirty years, the British War Office opened the classified files concerning World War II. A serious reader of these descriptions of "war by other means" may feel inclined to revise his entire concept of what happened in World War II.[6]

The evidence was clear that the outcome of visible conflict depended upon highly subjective evaluations of intentions, capabilities, and behavior that would be invisible to all except those involved. This behavioral component of strategy is fundamental to its development and its execution. All of the developments, insight, and theories of strategy up until 1975 were useful but merely part of a jigsaw puzzle in which the relationships of the parts were still unknown.

The advantage of hindsight may someday cause business historians to feel that 1975 was the turning of the tide: the beginning of the integration of a general theory of strategy and competition. In 1975 Edward O. Wilson, a Harvard professor, published a landmark book entitled *Sociobiology*. In this book he attempted to synthesize all that is known about population biology, zoology, genetics, and social behavior. The resulting foundation of a conceptual framework was based on the social behavior of species that were successful because of that behavior. Since the whole structure of the biological community is determined by competition for resources, this kind of analysis has many parallels for business.

Mankind as a species is at the top of the ecological chain but is still a member of the biological community. Economics is only a subset of the behavior pattern of this species. Alfred Marshall pointed this out in his 1920 text, *The Principles of Economics*, when he said, "Economics has no near kinship with any physical science. It is a branch of biology broadly interpreted."

Wilson's synthesis is the closest approach to a general theory of competition that has yet been achieved. Business competition is a specialized form of this but nevertheless is subject to the same principles and is part of the same conceptual framework. The parallels may lead to a further insight into a general theory of business competition, such as the one proposed by Jack Hirshleifer:

> There is, however, a special link between economics and sociobiology over and above the mere fact that economics studies a subset of the social behavior of higher mammals. The fundamental organizing concepts of the dominant analytical structures employed in economics and in sociobiology are strikingly parallel.

The traditional core of compartmentalized economics is characterized by models that:

- postulate rational self-interest behavior on the part of individuals who have preferences for goods and services; and
- attempt to explain these interactions among such individuals through the form of market exchanges under a fixed legal system of property and free contract.

Only a very limited portion of human behavior can be adequately represented by such self-imposed constraints. In recent years economics has begun to break through these self-imposed barriers.

> From one point of view the various social sciences devoted to the study of mankind, taken together, constitute but a subdivision of the all encompassing field of sociobiology.[7]

The factors of sociobiological analysis have proceeded so far that much of the results of research has become quite suitable for computerized analysis. There is considerable promise that within the next generation or so these sociobiological factors can be so well defined and quantified that analysis can be far more predictive than ever before. This is the hope and expectation that Wilson holds out.

The mathematical descriptions of niches by Hutchinson in 1958, Levins in 1963, and McArthur in 1968, 1970, and 1972 made the analysis of niches quantitative. These authors considered a resource spectrum with the niche for each species defined by its utilization function distribution along the axis of the resource it consumes.

Biological study of competition has a long history. But that history was punctuated with a flash of brilliant insight in 1859 by Darwin and Wallace, and then followed by more than three-quarters of a century of data gathering, and apparently little progress, until all of this knowledge began to come together in the third quarter of the twentieth century.

When Darwin delivered his paper, *On the Origin of Species*, to the Royal Academy of Science in London in 1859, it was a perspective from a mountain peak. It would be a long time before the outlines would be examined in detail.

But some of his remarks can readily be translated from biological competition to business competition:

> Some make the deep-seated error of considering the physical conditions of a country as the most important for its inhabitants; whereas it cannot, I think, be disputed that the nature of the other inhabitants, with which each has to compete is generally a far more important element of success.

> When we reach the arctic regions, or snowcapped summits, or absolute deserts, the struggle for life is almost exclusively with the elements. . . . When we travel southward and see a species decreasing in numbers, we may feel sure that the cause lies quite as much in other species being favored, as in this one being hurt.

> As species of the same genus have usually, though by no means invariably, some similarities in habits and constitution, and always in structure, the struggle will generally be more severe between species of the same genus, when they come into competition with each other, than between species of distinct genera.

The biologists began to focus on relationships between species in the mid-twentieth century. There are millions of species. They are all unique in their particular niche. This very fact raises the question about the nature of the forces that keep them in equilibrium with each other. Inevitably there is perpetual competition because many species use the same resources. In addition many of the resources for one specimen are other species below them in the ecological chain.

Gradually a whole series of patterns of behavior and characteristic relationships emerged from this intensive research. The analogies to business competition are striking. In the absence of strategy, it *is* biological competition. As Marshall and Hirshleifer pointed out, economics is only a subset of the sociobiology of one species of the primates. However, the ability to use strategy is the ability to manage the natural competitive system by calculated intervention in order to produce predictable shifts in competitive equilibrium. For that to be possible, you must first understand the characteristics of natural competition.

Natural competition in the strict sense, as it is defined by Darwinian natural selection and evolution, contains no element of strategy. It is pure expediency; almost mindless at some stages. Instinctive needs that are urgent serve as the motivation. Day-to-day survival and cyclical procreation are the ultimate objectives.

This kind of competition by natural selection is glacially slow. It is trial and error. More mistakes than improvements will prove to be fatal. Over time the more successful patterns must be immortalized and multiplied by the genes, while the mistakes must be diminished in future generations by the same process. It must be a slow process to succeed at all.

Natural competition can and does evolve exquisitely complex and effective forms eventually. Mankind itself is such an end result. But unmanaged change takes many thousands of generations. Sometimes, perhaps often, change is too slow to cope with the combination of a changing environment and the adaptation of competitors.

Time Compression by Strategy

By contrast, strategic competition is revolutionary, not just evolutionary. It is capable of extreme time compression. However, to accomplish this revolution, the preparation must be conservative, careful, precise, and all inclusive. The environment itself must be well understood. The competitors who are critical or even important to the change must be equally well identified and understood. Then uncertainties in the environment must be carefully assessed and evaluated. The systematic interaction of competitors with each other and the environment must be modeled and tested for sensitivity. This meticulous staff work must be continued until cause and effect become sufficiently predictable to justify the massive commitment of non-recoverable resources.

The wild expediency of natural competition leads to glacial evolution. The meticulous conservatism of strategic competition leads to time compression and revolutionary change because strategy is the management of natural competition.

The biological model of natural competition provides illustrations of relationships that are important in business competition:

• Every species (business) must be uniquely superior to all others in its chosen combination of characteristics that define its competitive niche or segment.

- The boundaries of a competitive niche are determined by the points where competitors are equivalent.
- At any given boundary line, there will always be a specific competitor who determines that boundary.

The number of boundary competitors is determined by the number of possible tradeoffs between behavioral characteristics and capabilities that will provide a differential advantage over other competitors in that environment.

There are a number of corollaries:

- The more variable the environment, the more combinations that may become critical.
- The more distinctly different resources needed, the more possible critical combinations that exist.
- If any one factor is overwhelmingly important, only one competitor will survive.

If the biological pattern of natural competition is useful as a model, then the reality of the competitive system is quite different from traditional microeconomic models.

- Every competitor, whatever its role in the competitive system, requires certain resources to persist.
- In the absence of some constraint on those resources, every competitor would tend to grow to infinity.
- In almost every case the limit on growth or size is set by the ability of some competitor to preempt a significant part of the supply.
- No two competitors can coexist who make their living in the same way. Their relationship is unstable. One will displace the other. This is Gause's Principle of Mutual Exclusion.
- Except for the most elementary forms of life, the required resources are other forms of life or activity. This establishes a form of vertical equilibrium. The higher levels prey on the lower levels but cannot live without them. Excessive success is self-defeating.
- The horizontal competition between organisms or organizations combined with the vertical dependency on an ecological chain constitutes a community or web of relationships that is in dynamic equilibrium but in which competition in all dimensions is perpetual.

- A stable relationship that permits both competitors to coexist requires each competitor to have a combination of characteristics in some segment or sector of the environment that permits it to be uniquely superior in that "competitive segment."
- The source of virtually all resources is elementary natural material. The conversion of these to the form of end use must necessarily be an ecological chain in which each link is the resource for the next higher level that is dependent on the continuation of all the lower level links.

Some analogies between sociobiology and business lead to testable and reasonable hypotheses:

- Pure chance provides an initial advantage to the first competitor to enter or define a competitive segment. The initial competitor becomes a part of the environment to be coped with by the next competitor who chooses to enter that specific arena.
- Definition of a new competitive segment requires that the differences between the specific competitors involved be sufficient to provide a distinct advantage to one of the competitors compared to all others in the competitive niche that is erected.
- If competitors are alike and equally capable, they cannot coexist. One will displace the other.
- Competitors who have distinctly different capabilities cannot coexist in the same competitive segment, but they can and will be in perpetual competition along the boundary lines where their respective competitive segments come into contact (the line of zero advantage).
- If there are few competitors and the market is thin, then the generalist has the advantage. The generalist can obtain a small amount of resources from multiple sources, but the thin market will support a few specialists on an adequate scale to be effective competition for the generalist.
- Conversely, rich markets tend to eliminate generalists since the market can be subdivided into competitive segments, each of which can be dominated by specialists of significant scale and scope.
- The ability to grow rapidly when conditions are favorable, and to survive long periods of adversity when conditions are unfavorable, can be a critical combination that offsets superiority in many other respects if the environment is cyclical.

- Since size or scale often provides a significant advantage and size or scale is incompatible with many other characteristics, then an orderly distinction from small to large size is predictable when there is a diversity of factors that are important in a market or environment.

- Since distance and logistics are often critical factors, then both scale and total market size are factors that determine the number, size, distribution, and competitive segment boundaries where these factors are important.

- Since the variety of characteristics among competitors is matched by an equal or greater variety in desired or required resources, then every significant difference in customer preferences provides the possibility of subdivision into multiple competitive segments. This is dependent upon the capability to serve both segments simultaneously being incompatible with optimization of both.

- The characteristic fundamental resource segments for business are sources of:
  — money, either in capital or in ongoing revenue;
  — suitable skills, abilities, and individuals on an ongoing basis;
  — materials, supplies, energy, and components not contained within the organization; and
  — knowledge and communication capability with respect to all external resources and factors affecting their availability.

- Since multiple resources are always required, there will always be multiple competitors, each of which has characteristics that cause it to be the constraint on that specific resource availability.

- Each competitor for each resource will require a different combination of capabilities to be in stable equilibrium with competition.

- Adaptation to meet a specific competitor will often reduce the capability to offset another competitor.

- Any change in the environment will require adaptation of all competitors either to the environment or to each other or both. The equilibrium points between competitors will be shifted for all members of the community web of relationships.

   This is the logic that describes the competitive system's major constraints. The complexity should be obvious, since it is inherent in millions of unique competitors in a moving but stable dynamic equilibrium.
   Then for any specific individual competitor to use strategy, that competitor must be able to visualize the system's behavior and his own relationship to it.

The fundamental requirements for strategy development are:

- a critical mass of knowledge;
- the ability to relate this knowledge in the form of an interactive system;
- the capability of system analysis adequate to determine the probabilities of cause and effect for inputs that result in delayed higher order effects;
- the orderly analysis of alternatives and tradeoffs to determine the optimum sequence and timing of reallocation of available resources; and
- an adequate excess of resources beyond current needs to permit reallocation and the capability of tolerating deferral of benefits in order to compound them.

In business these basics must be converted into an analytical process that permits development of a specific strategy. There are a number of steps:

- First, self-examination to determine what is needed to achieve the organization's purposes and implicit goals. This will determine the combination of resources that will be required on a continuing basis.
- Second, determination of which competitors are the obstacles to those specific resources.
- Third, determination of the differences between you and each of those specific competitors that make each of you superior within your own competitive segments.
- Fourth, determination of which combinations of what factors produce those differences in capability.
- Fifth, mapping of the boundaries of "zero advantage" that determine the individual competitive segments.
- Sixth, mapping of the competitive characteristic resources, behavior patterns and alternatives.

At this point the strategy development process becomes highly analytical in an effort to assess the available alternative payoffs, risks, and odds. Because the possible combinations are nearly infinite, however, the final choice, like many business decisions, is essentially an intuitive one.

In spite of the enormous effort and attention devoted to this process, procedure and conceptual framework over the past twenty years, it is still very much in an early stage of development. The task is even more complex than it appears to be.

Almost every corporate organization is composed of multiple businesses. This requires multiple but compatible strategies. The strategies must be compatible because for a given company all the business units draw upon a common base of resources. The different businesses may share certain capabilities in a synergistic fashion or in an incompatible or preemptive fashion. The company as a whole may have purposes and goals that override or are incompatible with those of the units.

The defender of a competitive segment normally has a significant advantage if alert and entrenched. The result of this is usually a "cold war" stable equilibrium between most competitors. This kind of equilibrium is conditionally unstable—that is, stable unless disturbed beyond a certain point. Skirmishing and testing of limits occurs continually on the boundary line. Such a cold war stability depends on the acceptance by both parties that the odds of winning a hot war are insufficient to offset the inevitable losses and destruction of a "negative sum" payoff from such an escalation.

A company with multiple businesses has a multiple of the total resources available to a single business. However, it loses that advantage if the strategies of the individual businesses are not coordinated to preserve adequate uncommitted reserves if any individual business strategy contemplates escalation.

Strategy and the Future

Strategy development is still embryonic. But the rate of development of the conceptual base is rapid and holds forth the promise of precision, elegance, and power within a reasonable time period. Sociobiologist Wilson foresees the probability of the quantification of sociobiological behavior, even the computerization of analysis, within the next decade or so. In the same way, business strategy development should soon go through a period of rapid development. As this happens, the problems of strategy execution will emerge as even more formidable and challenging. Here, too, there is promise that sociobiology will provide guides that will compress the time of accomplishment.

It seems almost certain that exponential growth in insight with respect to business competitive strategy will result in time compression for change. Those companies who are not able to learn, adapt, and apply these emerging insights at an accelerated rate are subject to Darwinian natural selection. In this context, the race will be won by the swift.

Notes

1. All quotes from B. H. Liddell Hart, *Strategy* (New York: Praeger, 1954), pp. 164, 347, 365.
2. Oskar Morganstern and John von Neumann, *Theory of Games and Economic Behavior* (Princeton, NJ: Princeton University Press, 1953).
3. Jay W. Forrester, *Industrial Dynamics* (Cambridge, Mass: M.I.T. Press, 1961).
4. Bruce D. Henderson, *Perspectives on Experience* (Boston: The Boston Consulting Group, Inc., 1968).
5. The Conference Board, "Strategic Planning and the Future of Antitrust," (Bulletin No. 90, 1980).
6. See, for example, William A. Stevenson, *A Man Called Intrepid* (New York: Harcourt, Brace, Jovanovich, 1976); Anthony Cave Brown, *Bodyguard of Lies* (New York: Harper & Row, 1975); James M. Gavin, *On to Berlin* (New York: Viking Press, 1978).
7. Jack Hirshleifer, "Economics from a Biological Perspective," *Journal of Law and Economics*, 20:1 (1977).

2. STRATEGIC SECTORS

A strategic sector is one in which you can obtain a competitive advantage and exploit it. Strategic sectors are defined entirely in terms of competitive differences. Strategic sector analysis performs the same function as cost effectiveness analysis. Cost effectiveness analysis optimizes value relative to cost. Strategic sector analysis optimizes margin relative to competition.

Strategic sector analysis, like cost effectiveness analysis, ignores the administrative unit until the objective and its feasibility have been evaluated. The resources and the program component are assigned as necessary to administrative units in order to accomplish the mission.

Strategic sectors cut across the profit centers, strategic business units, groups, divisions, departments, markets, and all other administrative units. The boundary of a strategic sector is defined by the maximum rate of change of relative competitive margin as that boundary is crossed.

Strategic sectors exist because the same product can be made in many variations and supplied with many related services. Each feature and each service has a cost. But the value added by such increments varies from customer to customer. It affects product design, manufacturing capability, and distribution practices. Every change in these affects both cost and value simultaneously.

Design requires focus on the strategic sector to be served. Yet every compromise of that focus either adds cost or reduces value.

Manufacture requires focus on the strategic sector to be served. Compromises and variety produce the same consequences on cost and value. No job shop can match the cost of a full-scale focused factory. A given strategic sector can rarely use more than one distribution channel. Since different channels have different costs and provide different services, they appeal to different customers. Customers of one channel tend to be in a different strategic sector from those served by other channels. Competitors who try to serve both strategic sectors at the same price are handicapped by a too high price in one sector and a too high cost in the other.

Profit centers and strategic business units are self-defeating unless the whole company is the profit center. GM can be the most profitable competitor because the whole company is the business unit while internal administrative units are tailored to focus on value added in strategic sectors in which they can be the largest factor.

Profit centers originated when companies became too big and complex to manage by individual function. Decentralization, however, led to suboptimization and loss of internal financial mobility that is critical to strategic concentration.

Strategic business units were devised to reverse the effects of overfragmentation into profit centers. So-called SBUs attempted to aggregate all the strategy decisions in an administrative unit. The critical factor, cash flow, cannot be delegated to any SBU. If it is, then the parent is merely a lock-box holding company without strategic options as a company except divestment or acquisition. Strategic sectors are the key to strategy because the strategic sector's frame of reference is competition.

The very largest competitor in an industry can be unavoidably unprofitable if the individual strategic sectors are dominated by smaller competitors. Market share in the strategic sector is what determines profitability, not size of company.

3. THE STRATEGY TRADEOFF: MARKETING VERSUS MANUFACTURING

Every production man's dream is a factory that always runs at capacity making a single product that requires no change. Such a situation permits the minimum possible cost to be achieved, produces the least problems, and is the easiest to manage.

Every salesman would like to give every customer whatever he wants immediately. That would produce the maximum possible revenue, require the least sales effort, provide a competitive advantage, and be equal in value to a price cut.

These two extremes are incompatible regardless of cost or price. In the production version, every customer would be forced to take the same thing. There can be no options or variations without production changes and interruptions. Change and variety produce major inventory problems, particularly in seasonal businesses. Change and variety compound overhead by increasing the need for communication and control as well as investment in inventory.

Henry Ford's black Model T came the closest to the production man's ideal. It was the beginning of low-cost mass production. But Ford nearly went out of business when his attempt at a major model change shut down production for over a year. Even worse, Ford was unable to match his product to more than one segment of the total market. General Motors' market segmentation matched the market segments of the growing urban market while costs were controlled by component standardization.

An approach focused entirely on marketing is equally impractical if carried to extremes. Immediate delivery of variety is impossible without heavy finished stock inventory with all combinations of options. Complexity has a very high price in inventory costs alone. Every change in a schedule level has a high cost. Every variation in the composition of a schedule also has a cost. Every reduction in the lead time for delivery increases the cost of adjustment and reduces the possibility that the schedule will or can be met. Special short lead time orders disrupt the schedule on all other orders too. The indirect costs of complexity, variety, uncertainty, and intermittent operation are monumental.

Every maker of a family of products faces this problem. Dissimilar products made to customer specifications take time to order, to manufacture, and to deliver. They undermine the economies of scale and long-run lengths. They are expensive to make. The tradeoffs are legion: complexity versus simplicity, lead time versus variety, capacity versus flexibility, cost versus revenue. Mistakes in the tradeoffs are very costly.

Such tradeoffs between manufacturing cost and marketing determine both volume of sales and manufacturing cost. Their optimization as a combined system is fundamental to a successful competitive position.

Marketing Optimization

Optimization of marketing economics requires assessment of customer values and the ability to obtain a premium for superior matching of those values. This includes tradeoffs between how much, how many, and how long. This evaluation deals primarily with revenue generation and distribution costs.

How many more units will you sell if you have stock on hand for immediate delivery? How long will a customer wait to get exactly what he wants? How much more will a customer pay to get exactly what he wants compared to functionally equivalent alternatives? How much will he pay if he must also wait much longer?

Such questions are present in many customer choices. The existing house or the custom-built house? The car on the dealer's lot versus the car built to customer option specifications? The ready-to-wear suit versus the custom-tailored suit?

Manufacturing Optimization

Optimization of manufacturing economics requires evaluation of an equivalent set of questions involving indirect as well as direct costs of the marketing pattern. What is the real and total cost of complexity? What is the cost of schedule changes? What is the extra cost of short lead times or small lot production? What is the marginal revenue generated by an added sale in otherwise unused capacity? How much factory cost is created indirectly to service the short lead time schedule change?

Most products have some seasonal patterns of sales as well as patterns determined by business cycles. Is it possible to have a level loaded factory that runs evenly all year? Which is better: shortages at the height of the season or excessive inventory the rest of the year? If such a factory never has shortages, it must have finished stock inventory even at the seasonal peak. Most factories have a compromise that includes high inventories part of the time and long lead times for delivery part of the time.

The other alternative is the factory that produces as soon as possible but only on specific customer order. Such a factory must have substantial excess capacity for the peaks and substantial seasonal employment. This adds cost and quality problems. Anything else is a compromise with the level loaded factory.

System Optimization

Optimization of either marketing or manufacturing results in suboptimization for the company as a whole. The optimal evaluation, no matter how precise and analytical, must be finally resolved on the basis of relevance to corporate strategy, resources, and purposes. Such problems have been approached differently in the past by different producers and different cultures.

Certain of the European automobile manufacturers have characteristically had long lead times and few options. This was true of Volkswagen for some time in the 1950s. A few years ago the Mercedes was so scarce that employees added to their income by reselling their employee allotment to customers unwilling to wait a year for delivery.

The same shortage situation existed in the U.S. automobile market in the immediate post—World War II period. Automobile dealers became rich. The car manufacturers set price based on normal volume and cost. The dealers priced on supply versus demand.

Certain Scandinavian crystal and china have had long delivery times for many years. The factory work force is employed continuously at capacity. Only the backlog varies.

Even today Honda dealers in the United States are selling their available allotment at well above sticker prices to those who are unwilling to join a queue of several months' wait. The consumer price and the waiting time vary directly as a function of sales. The total available product does not vary. All Japanese car makers have chosen to limit their customer options in the export market and to a considerable degree in their domestic market. Most of their dealers have limited stock on hand. In part this choice may account for their generally accepted cost advantage, both at the factory and in their distribution system. Variety requires increased inventory with added financing cost, space, insurance, and obsolescence.

This has not inhibited their trend-line growth. Toyota is now the world's second largest automobile maker behind GM. Datsun is bigger than Ford. Toyo Kogyo (Mazda), Honda, and Mitsubishi make more cars than Chrysler. Japan has surpassed the United States in total automobile production with a far smaller home market and more competitors.

The difficulty in being logical and analytical in these tradeoffs between marketing and manufacturing is increasing. The Toyota Production System (TPS) has come into general use in Japan during the past five years. Its effective use provides substantial reduction in total manufacturing cost and capital employed. One fundamental policy is "just in time" (JIT) delivery of material required for each operation. Another is extremely rapid exchange of dies and tools in machine setups.

The first of these, JIT, requires progressively less flexible schedules for periods up to several months before actual output. The second, fast die exchange, greatly reduces the cost of manufacturing complexity and short runs, provided the rest of the system is properly tuned.

The implication of this is that the marketing organization will have to commit to a production schedule earlier but the cost of variety or product complexity will go down. The cost of any very short lead time schedule change goes up. But the cost of variety is reduced provided the schedules are stable.

Many markets are notoriously fickle. The automobile market is not an exception. Accommodation to shifts in style or model are not difficult with TPS scheduling, but shifts in total production level can make JIT scheduling difficult. This, however, must be weighed against the overall cost advantages conferred by TPS. The cost advantages almost make it a prerequisite to remain competitive in many kinds of manufacturing. Competitors without TPS who try to match variable demand are likely to have costs and therefore prices too high for even the most impatient customers.

There is a worldwide trend for all costs, including labor costs, to become fixed in most industrial countries. Normal labor turnover rates will gradually become the limit on how fast labor cost can be reduced regardless of output. Labor is in fact becoming as fixed a cost as capital equipment. This is particularly true for short time shifts in labor use because of schedule changes. The social pressures for labor stability are additional.

We may enter an era of far greater labor employment stability but perhaps much greater fluctuation in prices and delivery lead times. The fluctuations in margins this will produce will profoundly change the manufacturer/retailer/customer relationship just as TPS will profoundly change the manufacturer/supplier relationship. This development may be severely modified, however, by misguided antitrust or labor practices regulation.

Any overall approach to optimizing the complex tradeoffs of the machinery manufacturer must start with analysis of the most cost-effective manufacturing configuration for a given product. Henry Ford's black Model T was a basic reference in that sense. It had the minimum manufacturing cost for that product.

To optimize the tradeoffs, each variation in scheduling, in product complexity, in lead time, in lot size, in flexibility must be costed out in terms of overall cost to the whole system, both direct and indirect. Each of the variations must then be priced out in terms of marginal revenue, with or without the variation. Since many cost variables and revenue variables are covariables, there is no simple analysis.

The complexity of analysis is high because any starting point in fixed investment, labor force, and product mix may be far from the current optimum for either the individual maker or an entire industry. Even more complexity must be resolved to make the manufacturing and marketing strategies compatible and to optimize them. These are formidable tasks. But without such analysis, the competitive strategy must be based on hunch and rule of thumb.

The actual optimum strategy may be unconventional when compared with practices of the past. Yet the ability to adapt to the new challenges and opportunities may be the critical variable in competitive survival. The TPS/JIT techniques will narrow the cost spread between small and large corporations. It will also provide the smaller competitor a cost advantage and additional strategy options if everyone does not adopt the same practices. The smaller competitor who prices on marginal cost when his schedule lead time begins to get short can become a truly formidable competitor.

If all kinds of competitors begin to adopt these practices, then lead times or prices or both will fluctuate more widely on consumer goods. If that becomes a widespread practice, the production levels of producer goods will become less cyclical than in the past. The end market price and values will be the swing variable instead of the manufacturing output level. Will companies let their capacity growth lag the demand for their products? The TPS/JIT techniques tend to increase capacity steadily without increase in floor space or employment. The increased cost advantage may well exceed the marginal revenue or the scale effects of competitors whose capacity additions lead their sales.

Those who can understand the economics of such a cost benefit/production marketing system will have a substantial competitive advantage. Those who can convert this into an appropriate strategic response first will tend to displace those who are unable to follow their lead. If all this happens, we will all win because our personal productivity will be higher, prices will be lower, and our variety of choices will be greater. We will also be strongly motivated to change some of our buying habits as individuals, as well as our production scheduling as manufacturers.

4. STRATEGIC AND NATURAL COMPETITION

Strategic competition leads to time compression. Competitive shifts as a result of strategy can take place in a few short years. The same evolution by natural competition might require generations.

Strategic competition is a relatively new phenomenon in business. It may well have the same impact on business productivity that the industrial revolution had upon individual productivity.

The basic elements of strategic competition are:

- ability to understand competitive interaction as a complete dynamic system that includes interaction of competitors, customers, money, people, and resources;
- ability to use this understanding to predict the consequences of a given intervention in that system and how that intervention will result in new patterns of stable dynamic equilibrium;
- availability of uncommitted resources that can be dedicated to different uses and purposes in the present even though the dedication is permanent and the benefits will be deferred;
- ability to predict risk and return with sufficient accuracy and confidence to justify the commitment of such resources; and
- willingness to deliberately act to make the commitment.

This description of strategy sounds like the basic requirements for making any ordinary investment. It is that, but it is far more. Strategy is all-encompassing in its commitment. Strategy by definition involves the commitment and dedication of the whole firm. Failure of any competitor to react and then deploy and commit his own resources against the strategic competition of another competitor can result in a complete inversion of the competitive relationships and a major shift in the equilibrium between them. That is why strategic competition leads to time compression. Natural competition has none of these characteristics.

Natural competition is wildly expedient in its moment-to-moment interaction. However, it is inherently extremely conservative in its change in characteristic behavior. By contrast strategic competition is deliberate, carefully considered and tightly reasoned in its commitments, but the consequences may well be radical change in a relatively short time.

Natural competition is evolutionary. Strategic competition is revolutionary.

Natural competition is really low-risk incremental trial and error. Small changes that seem to be beneficial are gradually adopted and maintained. Other small changes are tried and added. It is learning by trial and error without the need for either commitment or foresight. It is the adaptation to the way that things are now. It is the basic pattern of evolution. It is Darwinian natural selection. It functions even if controlled by pure chance or pure expediency. For these very reasons it is inevitably conservative and gradual and produces nearly imperceptible near-term change regardless of the ultimate long-term consequences.

Strategic competition by its commitments seeks to make a large change in competitive relationships. Its revolutionary character is moderated only by two fundamental inhibitions. Strategic failure can be as sweeping in its consequences as strategic success. And characteristically an alert defense has a major competitive advantage over the attacker. Strategic success usually depends upon the culture, perceptions, attitudes, and characteristic behavior of competitors and their mutual awareness of each other.

This is why in geopolitics and in military strategy as well as in business strategy the pattern of competition contains long periods of natural competition punctuated by relatively sudden and major shifts in relationships as a result of strategy. It is the age-old pattern of war and peace even though competition continues during peace.

Currently normal modern business behavior seems to fall between the extremes of these two modes. However, a shift toward strategic competition seems to be the secular trend. The successful use of strategic competition by the most aggressive direct competitor can make the same foresight and dedication of resources the prerequisite for survival of others. Eventually the mastery of strategic competition will be a requirement for adapting to that kind of environment in which most of the change is the result of strategic commitments.

Natural competition should be respected. It is the process that produced the infinite and exquisite complexity, variety, and interaction of all the forms of life. This was accomplished by pure chance with no plan, foresight, or objectives: It started from the equivalent of sterile chemical soup and took millions of years of nearly infinitesimal changes and adaptations.

Natural competition must be completely understood. It is the foundation. It is the system and pattern of interaction upon which any form of strategic competition must build and modify. Natural competition must be understood in order to predict the effect of intervention in that system.

Differences between competitors is the prerequisite for survival in natural competition. Those differences may not be obvious. But competitors who make their living in exactly the same way in the same place at the same time are highly unlikely to remain in a stable equilibrium. However, any differences may give one competitor or the other an advantage over all others in some part of the common competitive environment. The value of that difference becomes a measure of the survival prospects as well as the future prosperity of that competitor.

There is nearly an infinite number of combinations of competitive factors in an environment that has a large number of variables. It should not be surprising that the world is filled with a vast variety of competitors, all different, that seem to exist in a moving but stable equilibrium. The range of size, behavior, and other characteristics is not accidental; it is inevitable. It is also stable even though changing in detail. Those differences are the a priori requirement for survival in a particular subsection of the environment. That is natural competition as it always has been.

Strategic competition is not new. The elements of it have been recognized and used in warfare since the human race combined intelligence, imagination, accumulated resources, and deliberately coordinated behavior. The distilled wisdom of centuries has been expressed in maxims such as "concentrate strength against weakness."

But most military strategy has focused on the battle or the war rather than on the equilibrium of the relationship that continued through both peace and war. Geopolitics is the larger perspective of the continued competition of this dynamic equilibrium over time. Yet there is still a very limited general theory about geopolitical dynamic equilibrium.

The general theory of business competition is almost certainly in its infancy. But the elements of a general theory that integrates all of the elements seem to be developing. The integration itself is the critical development.

The classic economic theories of business competition are so simplistic and sterile that they have become obstacles to progress and understanding rather than contributions. They seem to be based on views of competition as a static equilibrium in a static economy rather than a dynamic equilibrium. They are based on theoretical concepts of cost behavior that have never been observed in reality and that directly contradict observable and quantifiable evidence. They make assumptions about competitive behavior that are neither observable nor useful in predicting competitive behavior. The frame of reference of "perfect competition" is a theoretical concept that has never existed and probably could not exist. Unfortunately they have been used to develop equally unrealistic public policy.

Development of the general theory of business competition will permit the prediction of the consequences of any kind of business competition. It can be the base of both strategic competition and constructive public policy. The general public would benefit on both counts. The development of a general theory of business competition will require the testing and revision of many interlocking hypotheses.

We would now hypothesize that:

- Effective competitors will result in a range of sizes of competitors from very large to very small. This spectrum of size will be stable over time.
- Competitors who survive and prosper will have unique advantages over any and all other competitors in specific combinations of time, place, products, and customers.
- For any given competitor, there will be different competitors who will provide the constraints for almost every combination of relevant factors. Therefore the frontiers or boundaries of competitive parity will be constantly changing as any one of the competitors changes, adapts, grows, or redeploys.
- Perpetual conflict will exist along those frontiers where competitive ability is at parity.
- Very little conflict will exist where clear superiority is visible. The military analogy of the battle front is useful in visualizing this.
- Business competition is inherently multiple front with a different competitor on each front.
- Any redeployment of resources will change the balance of competitive parity on at least two fronts. If one is strengthened, others will be weakened.
- Whenever a front or zone of competitive parity becomes stable or static, then "bourgeois" competition will develop. Such "bourgeois" competition exists when the defense always acts as a hawk and the offense always acts as a dove. This is a mutual recognition of mutually predictable behavior.
- The fewer the number of critical competitive variables, the fewer the number of competitors. If only one factor is critical, then no more than two or three competitors are likely to coexist. Only one will survive if the available market shrinks. This is the "rule of three and four."
- The greater the number of important variables, the larger the number of competitors that will coexist, but the smaller will be their absolute size.
- The more variable the environment, the fewer the number of surviving competitors. In this case, the ability to cope with the greater change in environment becomes the overriding and controlling factor.
- The new entry or the development of a new competitor depends on the ability of that competitor to develop and identify a clear superiority compared to all other existing competitors in some subsection of the total market. Sequence of entry is important.

These and other hypotheses are direct derivatives from the observable facts and generally accepted theories of evolution in the biological and ecological sense. They are the pattern of natural competition.

The earlier work of The Boston Consulting Group attempted to develop a general theory of competition based on:

- observable patterns of cost behavior;
- considerations of the dynamics of sustainable growth and capital use;
- the role of the capital markets in permitting these effects to be leveraged or discounted; and
- the relationship between these in a system of competition.

We recognized early the inappropriateness of accounting theories developed for other purposes as a model of economic behavior. We then developed the concepts that can be summarized as "cash in and out is all that counts."

From this start, the concepts of the experience curve, the growth share tradeoff, and the product portfolio were developed. This was further extended by analysis of shared experience, business risk versus financial risk tradeoffs, the cost of proliferation, and cultural and behavioral extrapolation for competitors. Many of these ideas are now commonly accepted assumptions and part of the business language.

This conceptual framework of business competition is far from complete. Knowledge of competitive systems is expanding at an exponential rate, paralleling the expansion of our knowledge of the physical sciences in the last century. We believe that insight into strategic competition has the promise of a quantum increase in our productivity and our ability to both control and expand the potential of our own future.

5. CORPORATE STRATEGIES IN AN UNCERTAIN ECONOMY

There is nothing very unusual about strategy in an uncertain economy. As long as I can remember, the economy has always been uncertain.

But the most uncertain thing about our economy is whether we will be permitted to continue to exist as private corporations in a competitive market economy or whether we will be forced to live in a regimented, monolithic, totalitarian, controlled economy. The trend is ominous. In my opinion, our failure to really understand and explain the true nature of competition has substantially contributed to this trend.

A talk before The Corporate Development Institute Seminar *"Corporate Development Strategies in a Slowing Economy"* at the Plaza Hotel, New York, March 5, 1979

At present, many people fear another round of ever higher inflation with an even more severe depression. This is possible, but it has little to do with strategy unless it changes relative competitive capability after the depression is over. The whole base for strategy is long-term competitive differences.

For reasons that are unclear, most American businessmen have an acute inhibition about focusing on the specific competitors who are their constraints. Part of this is the result of antitrust law. Almost everything that concerns recognizing direct competition has been given a pejorative connotation. However, economists have provided little or no insight into the realities of competition. Their assumptions do not match reality nor have they been confirmed by observation.

Their view of competitive interaction is simplistic. The myth of the perfect market has been preserved in the fantasy of identical small competitors competing in a commodity market without inhibitions. That is not real. Nor is it useful as a concept or for decision rule formulation.

I see the world of competition from a quite different perspective. I would call it natural competition. This concept can be summarized in a few precepts:

- The whole world is the relevant market.
- The market is the sum total of its individual segments.
- No two competitors can coexist who make their living in the identical way.
- Market segments must be defined in terms of the differences between competitors.
- The value of competitive differences is determined by the characteristics of the available market.
- The effective difference between competitors is the net result of each and every difference of each and every kind.
- A market segment is a combination of customers and products or services with respect to which a given competitor has an advantage against all other competitors.
- Every competitor dominates his own segment or becomes extinct.
- There is no advantage at the segment boundary: Competition is perpetual.
- The boundaries of every segment are constantly shifting as the competitors adapt to compete with each other in a constantly shifting environment (the Red Queen syndrome).

All this seems obvious or simple. It fits the observable facts. It explains growth rates, profit levels and cash flow. It also supplies a reasonable frame of reference for explaining the facts of life and competition in all of their complexity. But more important than any of this is the potential for predicting the consequences of competition.

- It is possible to predict with confidence that the size and number of competitors will follow a quantifiable pattern.
- It is possible to predict that if a single factor is the critical one for a given market area, then only one, two, or three competitors will survive.
- It is possible to predict that benign, stable, but varied market characteristics will lead to finer and finer subdivisions into segments based on smaller and smaller competitive differences.
- It is possible to explain why this subdivision causes mature markets to be less profitable.

The universe of competition follows the laws of nature.

Competition includes behavioral factors as well as mathematical probabilities. Try your hand at poker if you doubt that. Poker is a strategy game that combines both chance and behavior with partial knowledge of both.

Behavioral patterns must control competition. If every competitor fought to win without regard to cost, soon there would be only one survivor. Such victories would, on balance, be highly destructive. All continued competition that stabilizes with multiple competitors surviving must by definition lead to stalements where each decides to restrain competition beyond a certain level of effort or commitment.

If competition does not result in natural selection of the most productive competitor, then competition is destructive. Yet all competitive effort has a cost. If the benefits do not outweigh the cost of the competition, then we are all losers. Competition and competitors survive over time only because successful competitors put voluntary constraints on the degree of their competitive commitment.

We defined each competitor's segment as the matching of customers and products or services with respect to which that competitor has an advantage related to any other competitor. That means that at the boundary of every segment no one has an advantage. Then why fight there?

No one would attack if they believed the odds were steadily against them breaking even. Yet obviously if fighting always has a cost for both competitors, neither party will attack unless he believes the odds are in his favor. So when competition reaches equilibrium, it is always a stalemate in a static situation. But no boundary is ever really static.

- A competitor may weaken one boundary of his segment by concentrating his resources against a perceived weak point in a competitor's boundary. Such perceptions are basic to most strategy design.
- At different times the value of winning, or the cost of losing, may substantially shift temporarily.
- Consistent and therefore predictable strategy is rarely a favorable pattern of behavior.
- The odds may steadily shift because the market itself is changing.
- The odds may shift because of the characteristic willingness of a competitor to withdraw rather than risk escalation.
- The odds may shift because a competitor's characteristic behavior may be to always escalate without limit if directly confronted with an attack.

Each competitor who succeeds gradually evolves a culture that dictates a characteristic pattern of defensive and aggressive behavior. That pattern is characteristically a reinforcement of the behavior patterns that worked best when out-performing competitors in the past. That behavior pattern is as much a competitive characteristic as cost or product or customer focus.

Most of the things we have described above have been drawn from real life experience and natural selection. The largest and the most formidable competitors developed as they are by natural selection. So did the smallest. That natural selection was the survival of the fittest for a given segment that would support that kind of competition. The factors involved included behavioral characteristics and chance. The end result was the accumulation of all these things and an endless series of opportunistic ad hoc choices and decisions of individuals. But this was not a strategy, no matter now impressive the results. Natural selection and adaptation are based on wildly opportunistic expediency.

A strategy involves foresight, commitment of resources, coordination of efforts, and analysis that go far beyond the intuition and conditioned reflexes of the ad hoc expediency of day-to-day competition. All this may sound highly theoretical. It is not. It is the real world. The concepts have been developed and proven in the world's largest laboratory. The experiments have been going on for countless generations. It is true, however, that only in the last few decades have we been able to integrate this knowledge into a cohesive, tightly reasoned conceptual framework.

The laboratory is the earth itself. The experiment is, of course, the origin of living species. The time span is 3.5 billion years. The conceptual framework has been named the synthetic theory of evolution. The theoreticians are many but include Darwin, Mendel, von Neumann, Morgenstern, Lorenz, and a legion of scholars. The integrated material ranged from microbiology to the theory of games. The parallels between natural competition and business competition do not constitute proof. They are compelling circumstantial evidence that we do not really understand business competition, but that we can and soon:

- The food supply of the world in nature is the analogue of the total market in business.
- The niche for a species is the segment for a business competitor.
- The Darwinian fitness factor of a species is the growth rate of the business segment.
- The trophic levels of predators are the distribution chain of nonintegrated supply lines.
- The "population thinking" of a gene pool is the adaptive capability of a corporate culture.
- The "territorial imperatives" of biology are the bourgeois pattern of competitive escalation in game theory.
- The expediency of the profit center on a monthly profit budget has its parallel in the daily search for food of every living creature.

The parallels are breathtaking, but they have limits. Natural evolution by its very nature is inherently required to be extremely gradual. The increment of change must be small. There can be no coordination of change or investment in the future nor planning for higher order effects.

This is both the challenge and promise of the future for business. A similar natural selection in business has produced the extraordinarily complex and productive structure that makes the business world what it is today. But it does not have to evolve that slowly in the future.

Natural selection took quite a few million years to develop the first mammal that could fly, the bat. The Wright brothers integrated a critical mass of knowledge, and man first flew at Kitty Hawk only seventy five years before man flew to the moon, landed, and then flew back to earth. Man learned to fly and became the most powerful flyer of them all within a single man's life span. It was made possible by accumulating a critical mass of knowledge and then *investing* in a coordinated system designed to achieve a specific result.

Strategy offers the same potential for time compression that system design does compared to natural selection. However, insight into the dynamics of competition can produce the same discontinuity and quantum change in ability in business that it did in man's ability to fly.

Most business as it exists today is the result of natural selection by *natural competition*. The accomplishments, scale, and complexity of business as it exists today may be awesome. However, those accomplishments represent more natural selection, intuition, expediency, and chance than they do an integrated strategy. An integrated strategy has certain prerequisites:

- a critical mass of knowledge;
- an understanding of the system of competition;
- an assessment of alternatives over a substantial time span;
- focus on specific objectives;
- a plan;
- coordinated investment; and
- competitive intelligence.

The knowledge of competition and business economics has reached a critical mass. The future can change at an exponential rate of change. How do you compete in an uncertain economy? Learn how to understand competition better. Apply what you know in a focused investment based on an integrated strategy.

6. RESEARCH AND CORPORATE STRATEGY: HIT AND RUN

It is obvious that there are only two routes to leadership in a specific product market. You can invent the product and start with 100 percent of the market. Alternately, you can take the market away from the competitor who first dominated it.

There is an underlying business philosophy implicit in a business strategy that is dependent on invention.

This philosophy produces a sequence of:

— Invent.
— Skim the cream with high profit margins.
— Lose cost differential.
— Abandon.
— Replace with a new invention.

This pattern can be described more specifically in terms of a competitive product life cycle:

— The inventor establishes a high initial profit margin on 100 percent of the relevant market. The market grows rapidly. He has far lower costs than potential competitors.

— The profit margin and growth attract competition as soon as patent protection expires or licenses become available.

— Competitors price to penetrate the market. Their growth is faster than the pioneer's, but since their volume is small, the pioneer still grows while attempting to maintain the price level.

— The pioneer maintains margins but loses market share. Competitors' relative costs decline much faster as they grow faster.

— Eventually the faster growth of competitors more than absorbs all of the industry growth creating unused capacity. The pioneer's efforts to maintain existing facility operations at normal levels or to grow produce a declining price level for everyone.

— Overcapacity and declining price continue until capacity additions are discouraged. Characteristically, some producer does continue to add capacity and preempts most of the growth. The pioneer characteristically regards the product as a "commodity" long before this point is reached and therefore slows further investment of his own.

— Eventually the principal survivor, who usually is not the pioneer, has a dominant share of a product-market that is growing slowly by then. The costs of this survivor decline as market share grows (i.e. the experience curve effect). Profit margins tend to be highly satisfactory if it has an adequate lead in market share.

This dominant survivor has a profitable business that is almost immune to normal competition. Past experience has discouraged competitive interest. The by-now slow growth makes it difficult for a competitor to grow rapidly by preempting industry growth; the remaining competitors have higher costs. His own profit margin can be safely leveraged, giving a high return on shareholder equity.

As long as this principal survivor is content with a cash throw-off equal to cost differential, he has great security. He can set a price level that will make competitive investment unattractive and still provide net cash generation that continues to grow indefinitely at a modest rate. Only a significant mistake on his own part is apt to threaten his profit margin or market position thereafter.

STRATEGIC CONCEPTS   43

His profit is a function of his relative market share in the relevant segments.

Many competitors seem to have an interest only in the R&D and high margin portion of this cycle. This security of a stable, secure, and rewarding profit margin and position in a "commodity" seems to be of little attraction to them. Their emphasis on current profit margin rather than market share maintenance accelerates such a cycle.

This pattern has developed at an increasing rate in recent years. When competition reduces a product to a "commodity" in a short time span, then much of the value of research investment is effectively cancelled by the inability to capitalize on R&D long enough. The pioneer's investment in R&D becomes high risk accordingly. Such a product cycle is inherently high risk for *all* competitors.

Late entries into a product begin with an inherent cost disadvantage. To grow, they must invest heavily at a low or negative profit margin. For them, the investment must always be justified by hope of future profit instead of current return. There is always the risk that the leader—with lower costs—will prefer holding share to holding margin. If that happens before costs become equivalent, then the challenger's entire investment becomes nearly worthless. This risk is unavoidable for the follower who buys share from the innovator.

For the pioneer the risk is high too. Failure to continually produce new products will result in gradual liquidation of the firm. If product profitability life becomes too short, then the investment in research becomes a cost burden instead of a source of competitive advantage.

In this pattern of competition, the pioneer bets the company on its ability to continually produce new high margin products. If loss of share is too fast or the rate of new product introduction is inadequate, then the company's growth and profitability will both inevitably decline.

7. LIFE CYCLE OF THE INDUSTRY LEADER

Companies that are pioneers develop great technical expertise. This is valuable to customers, particularly in the early stages of the development of the customer's own expertise. It is a source of great pride and it is considered to be proof of leadership. This reinforces emphasis on technical development, and technical pride leads to tailoring each order to the optimum specification.

This in turn leads to the evolution of a manufacturing organization which is geared to produce a very wide variety. Likewise, the marketing organization seeks out unusual and technically difficult orders where this kind of flexibility and excellence offers the greatest competitive advantage. This is where the wide profit margins are.

All these stages reinforce each other. The company's leadership and success reinforce the corporate culture. They preserve and strengthen this pattern of competition.

Almost all original leaders developed this way and prospered because they did. It is necessary. In the early stages of every product and every industry, customers must have this kind of service and resource. The leader is rewarded handsomely because his greater experience and scale result in proportionately lower costs (i.e. the experience curve effect).

However, as the market becomes very large, the leader comes under price pressure from much smaller and less well-equipped competitors. The problem usually appears first with the largest and most knowledgeable customers. They have become expert themselves. They buy product, not service.

Such sophisticated customers do not need the full range of technical services and manufacturing variety that are available. They begin to find smaller, less competent suppliers who can give them an acceptable product at a lower price. At this stage, such competitors are rarely profitable. However, since they are able to concentrate their experience in a particular sector, their costs come down rapidly in that sector and their competence in that sector increases rapidly.

This competition poses a serious problem for the original leader. Large markets always have a number of sectors that differ materially in needs and characteristics. The costs of serving these sectors differ widely, and it is often difficult to price in a fashion that reflects the differences in services actually rendered or available.

If prices are high enough to cover the cost of the most expensive services available, then large portions of the total market will be lost to the specialized competitors who provide limited services and price accordingly. These prices are too low to cover costs for those customers who need and use the specialized service. A price midway between the two is worse than either, since it has the handicaps of both.

Under these conditions, market leaders usually try to price to preserve their average margin. This accelerates their margin shrinkage because they tend to lose their volume base on price but to increase their proportion of high-service, high-cost technical output.

This trend, if continued, changes the whole character of the leader with respect to costs, product characteristics, price policy, growth rates, and kinds of market sectors served. He becomes a high-price, high-cost, low-volume specialist. If the problem is not recognized and dealt with explicitly, it leads first to unprofitable business and then to inability to compete except in low-volume, high-margin specialties. By then, survival requires specialization in certain sectors and abandonment of the balance.

If the problem and its roots are recognized early enough, however, leadership, volume, and profitability can be protected and preserved. But for this to happen, major changes in policy are required. These changes are to policies that are fundamentally different from those that brought early success. This is where most pioneers lose their leadership. Price policy, product scope, marketing focus, manufacturing method, and production system must be fundamentally altered. This is a complex problem:

- Identifying market segment costs is very difficult. Many of these costs are joint costs. If one segment is served, the cost is often incurred in all segments. There is an infinite number of possible combinations of services and customer characteristics.

- Prices cannot always reflect different costs for those who do and those who do not need a service. If prices are not parallel to costs in all sectors, then a competitor can concentrate on a sector in which he has either a price advantage or a cost advantage.

- Competitors' costs in different sectors are never equivalent, even if average costs are the same. Since expected profit margins control investment, these differences will tend to produce differential growth rates. But cost differences are increased by shift in market share caused by differing growth rates.

- Changing marketing focus is of little help unless manufacturing facilities and production methods are modified to take advantage of the change. Yet, optimization of one is often incompatible with optimization of the other.

- Modification of manufacturing to obtain the optimum cost in any segment may curtail or restrict the product line or the service capability and, therefore, shrink the volume and experience base overall.

- Marketing advantage, manufacturing costs, and volume potential are mutually dependent variables. Overall optimization depends on competitors' characteristics, sector by sector.

It is a rare pioneer or industry leader that successfully makes the transition from generalized excellence across the board to focused competition segment by segment against specific competitors. There are too many forces that work against this adjustment:

- Marketing, engineering, and manufacturing all tend to take the policies and present character of the other two as a given and permanent constraint.

- The competitive success in concentration on certain sectors tends to continually concentrate the remaining business in those sectors that are the most complex, the most specialized, the least repetitive, and therefore the least likely to permit future cost reduction based on experience. The more successful the company has been in the past, the more the entire structure and company tradition will tend to inhibit a change in style or concept of competition.

- In cyclical businesses, a few good years make everything seem all right. In the down cycle, the problems are blamed on business conditions.

- The management of such businesses, particularly publicly owned businesses, tend to be measured on near-term results. Major change in policy takes time, costs money, and does not demonstrate its value until long after the cost and effort are incurred. Management has a disincentive to change.

It is easy to understand why many pioneers and early leaders are displaced by lesser competitors.

The health and life cycle of the pioneer are determined by two factors. The first is his ability to recognize significant differences in customer segments and optimize his cost of serving each segment separately. The second is his appreciation of the cost value of experience that is common to more than one segment.

2 COSTS AND THE EXPERIENCE CURVE

1. WHY COSTS GO DOWN FOREVER

Costs go down forever if:

— The product remains the same;
— Investment addition continues as long as there is a net return greater than interest cost;
— Management is active and competent; and
— Effects of inflation are removed.

Any change in a product for the same identical end use and value makes it cost less or the change would not be made. Any change in the product that adds incremental value must be worth the incremental cost or the addition of value would be pointless. The cost of the change goes down forever, too, although from a different base and at a different rate.

The several reasons for cost decline are intertwined. The learning experience reduces the time to do a given operation; however, that saving soon fades as the time to make a given increment of improvement stretches out with accumulated experience. This learning effect is renewed each time the job is split into components by specialization. The increased rate of repetition must be balanced by increased volume, however, to make the specialization possible.

Increased specialization is possible only through increased volume. Increasing volume means growth. Without growth, cost decline does in fact slowly fade until it becomes imperceptible. Growth leads to increasing scale, unless dissipated among many varieties or many competitors. The benefits of scale are easily observed: The labor required to control and maintain a large-scale facility does not increase as fast as the size, nor does the capital required.

These scale relationships can be approximated by the six-tenths rule. "Capital required varies as the six-tenths power of the capacity." This is a rule of thumb, but it closely correlates with observed experience that costs decline about 25 percent each time experience doubles. If experience doubles with volume and scale doubles with volume, then this rule of thumb coincides with the observable experience curve effect on cost decline. Any steady-state growth rate will in fact mathematically increase experience and volume at the same rate.

Any kind of growth requires added capital investment. The amount of capital committed is a function of the minimum acceptable return. The higher that minimum, the less the capital that can be employed. Yet any net return on capital after interest equivalent is a reduction of cost. Therefore, only when the cost of added capital exceeds the reduction in cost has the minimum total cost been achieved.

The scale effect alone should generate a 33 percent return on added investment when scale is doubled if only three-quarters of the capital per unit is required. (See Table 2−1.) Costs in real terms, for equivalent value to the user, should go down forever in real terms. But that cost decline will slow in proportion to slowing of growth. And it will not occur as it should unless each of the required actions is taken:

• Specialization increases with growth in scale;
• Capital is substituted for labor wherever there is a net return;
• Activity is concentrated to fully use the scale effect;
• Product change is avoided unless the incremental value is worth more to the user than the incremental cost; and
• New technology is not adopted unless the added value justifies the cost of changeover. Technology is just another form of investment where present cost compounds future output per unit of effort.

Product modification, feature addition, specialization, and product line extension do increase cost and add value. The tradeoffs of value added and cost added are exquisitely complex. Many cost elements share their scale and

Table 2-1.   The Scale Effect on Added Investment When Scale Is Doubled.

Capacity	Total Capital Employed		Total Capital Capacity
C	$C^{.6}$	k	
100	15.85 × 6.31	= $100	$1.00
200	24.02 × 6.31	= 151	.75
400	36.41 × 6.31	= 229	.57
800	55.19 × 6.31	= 348	.44
1600	83.65 × 6.31	= 521	.33

experience as common parts for many products. A change in activity for one product changes the cost reduction potential for all products that have shared cost elements. The market size itself is affected by the cost level and the consequently required price level.

Optimizing design and cost tradeoff is at best a complex, almost intuitive evaluation. This is particularly true when all costs are subject to the same forces, not just manufacturing costs. Yet the basic principle is simple and unchanged. It is observable everywhere and in every field. If management is competent, if capital is fully used, if customer needs are basic (and therefore stable)—*costs go down forever.* If this were not so, we could not continue to increase our per capita productivity.

2. THE EXPERIENCE CURVE REVISITED

In 1966 The Boston Consulting Group presented the concept of the experience curve. Since that first presentation, it has become commonly accepted as a real and important phenomenon. Acceptance has been impressive. So has the degree of oversimplification. Its application and limitations have been repeatedly misunderstood.

The experience curve is a rule of thumb. Its characteristic pattern is observable. "Costs of *value added* net of inflation will characteristically decline 25 to 30 percent each time the total accumulated experience has been doubled." (This plots as a straight line when plotted on logarithmic coordinates.)

That is all that the concept of the experience curve says. Everything beyond that is an inference, a hypothesis, a corollary, or a theory. Its implications are significant. It is pragmatic. It is a trend line. It is almost universally observable if looked for. Failure to find it is almost always a warning that there is a reason worth investigating.

The experience curve is a cost relationship. Prices may not parallel cost for long periods of time. In the United States prices parallel costs in only approximately two-thirds of the cases. In the other third there is usually a long period when prices stay unchanged in current dollars while costs decrease steadily. This is then followed by a long period of prices falling faster than cost. This pattern usually is accompanied by significant shifts in the market share and leadership. For some reason this unstable pattern rarely occurs in Japan. In Japan prices seem to parallel costs from the beginning in almost all situations.

Each element of cost in an end-product experience curve goes down its own independent cost curve. Each such element has its own separate starting point. The slope of each element may be different. Each cost element may share experience with other end products. The aggregation of these elements will not necessarily produce a straight line on logarithmic coordinates. The experience curve is necessarily an approximation of a trendline.

The cost characteristics of experience curves can be observed in all elements of cost—whether labor costs, advertising costs, overhead costs, marketing costs, development costs, or manufacturing costs. It seems to be immaterial whether the value added is labor or capital intensive.

Cost derivatives of the experience curve are not based on accounting costs. Accounting defers recognition of costs until revenue is realized. The experience curve is derived by dividing the accumulated cash input by the accumulated end product output. The cost decline of the experience curve is the rate of change in that ratio.

Experience per se is not the controlling factor. It is very difficult to have scale and not have volume or to have volume without accumulating experience. Constant rates of growth in volume produce close approximations of the same growth rate in accumulated experience.

Any explanation of the experience curve is a hypothesis. However, scale effects, the "learning curve," capital investment returns, substitution effects, critical mass of knowledge, and specialization are far more than enough to explain the observed characteristics of evolutionary, ever-declining costs with a constant trendline.

Differentials in market share do not fully reflect the implied cost differences when the experience of an entire industry is used as a reference. Individual competitors start at different times and have different growth rates, different cost slopes, and different shared experience. New competitors do not necessarily start at the same cost levels either. Typically, the "cross-section" curve at a point in time will show about half the cost differences that the difference in market share would cause you to expect.

The above statements are factual and not a matter of judgment. They have been verified by thousands of case examples.

It should be obvious that the definition of the product is critical to any use of this relationship. If you cannot define the product, then you cannot measure experience or even volume. The product must be defined in terms of perceived value to the customer or the definition is useless.

Often products change even though they serve the same needs of the same customers. This would not happen if the changed product was not more cost effective. Therefore, every product change that serves the same customers and the same needs results in a continuation of the experience cost curve for that product. Electronic watches replace mechanical ones, jet engines replace piston engines.

The same substitution phenomenon also applies to every cost element in a product: Adhesives replace lock washers, plastic milk cartons replace blended fiberboard, particle board replaces plywood, at least in some applications.

However, each of these substitutions changes the end-product characteristics enough so that the value of the end product has been shifted also. For some customers it has become more valuable; for others, less valuable. Therefore the market size, market potential, and market segmentation have all been shifted and readjusted.

These declines of cost elements are not uniform in rate. The electronic cost of a watch may decline much faster than the cost of its case; the cost of the case may decline faster than the marketing cost; and the marketing cost may go down faster than the overhead. Each of these shifts will be different in amount, timing, and importance for each competitor.

The experience curve cannot be a strategy or even the foundation for a strategy. It is merely a way to understand why and how competitive costs may shift.

Strategy is based upon competitive differences. If the experience curve permits you to confidently predict that one competitor can and should have a lower cost than another one, then the experience curve also permits you to predict that the low-cost competitor can and should displace the higher cost competitor if he provides identical products to identical customers with identical values at identical margins. That is the implication of the relationship between market share and the experience curve.

However, there is an ironclad law of competition: "No two competitors can coexist for very long who make their living in the same way." It is an observable fact that most companies make most of their profit from a very limited portion of their total business. It is less obvious but equally certain that most of the profit is earned where the competitive advantage is the greatest. This area of advantage is determined by both product characteristics and by customer characteristics. That is a competitively defined segment.

By that definition every successful competitor necessarily dominates his own segment, and that segment is the combination of customer and customer benefits over which he has a unique advantage.

Competitive segmentation and domination are observable, just as the experience curve is observable. They are facts. The whole object of strategy is to increase the competitive differentiation in a way that will increase both its absolute amount and its value in the marketplace.

Since all of these variations are distributed along a spectrum, the net result is an infinite number of gradations of net advantage in the competitive arena for every competitor. The severe competition always occurs along the boundaries of zero competitive advantage.

Simplistic interpretations of the experience curve can lead to faulty strategy. In the same way, simplistic interpretations of market share have led to both bad business strategy and bad public policy.

These misperceptions by competitors are strategy opportunities. The major unknown variable in strategy is the probable behavior and perceptions of competitors. If this were not true, all strategy would be merely an exercise in mathematical analysis. The ultimate creation of strategy depends on the commitment of resources and reserves as investments in the future. The interaction of "competitive segmentation" and "experience curves" can provide a powerful insight into the most critical strategy factor of all: competitor's behavior. Strategy is indirect, and it is not obvious even when all competitors know that there is a correlation between market share and cost.

3. THE EXPERIENCE CURVE: WHY DOES IT WORK?

"Cost of value added declines approximately 20 to 30 percent each time accumulated experience is doubled." This is an observable phenomenon. Whatever the reason, it happens. Explanations are rationalizations.

The whole history of increased productivity and industrialization is based on specialization of effort and investment in tools. So is the experience curve. It is a measure of the potential effect of specialization and investment.

Learning

Workers learn. If they learn to do a task better, they can do it in less time. This is equivalent to producing more in the same time. Characteristically, output can increase 10 to 15 percent each time total output is doubled. This is the well-known learning curve measure of man hour productivity increase. Based on the learning curve, labor costs should decline 10 to 15 percent each time accumulated experience doubles.

Specialization

When scale of activity increases so that numbers of people are involved, then it becomes possible to specialize. If two people are doing the same thing, it becomes possible to break the task into two parts. One person does all of one half; the other person does all of the other half. Each will therefore do his respective task twice as often for a given total output. The learning curve predicts that with twice the experience the labor time should be reduced 10 to 15 percent.

Increase in scale permits such specialization. Consequently, each worker will approach a total experience at any point in time that would be twice as much as he could have achieved without specialization. Doing half as much but twice as often equals the same amount of effort but twice the experience with the task. Consequently, specialization permits 10 to 15 percent less time per unit or 10 to 15 percent more output in a given time.

If the scale doubles simultaneously with total experience, then these two effects should occur simultaneously. Costs decline 10 to 15 percent because of learning plus 10 to 15 percent because of specialization. The sum of 20 to 30 percent cost decline is alone an approximation of the total experience curve effect. Where growth in output increases at any constant rate, then change in scale and change in total experience can and often do occur in parallel.

Investment

By definition, a profitable investment is one where money spent now results in a future payout that is larger than the original investment. All the return on investment comes in more output for the same total cost but deferred.

If the cost of money is extremely high, then virtually no investment can be justified. If the cost of money were zero, then any investment that would recover the investment and something more by eternity could be justified.

The cost decline in experience curves is a partial function of rate of investment. The control on this element is the cutoff rate on added investment. If the cutoff rate is high, costs decline slowly. If the cutoff rate is low, costs decline rapidly.

Return on investment does result in cost reduction. Without investment, capacity increase cannot occur and neither can cost reduction at constant capacity. A significant part of the experience curve cost reduction is the result of return on investment.

Scale

The experience curve effect is the result in part of increased scale. Yet there is no justification for increased scale unless there is growth. There is no need to add capacity at all.

With growth there is constant addition of capacity. Each added increment of unit capacity becomes a smaller percentage of the total capacity unless size of the increment is increased also. Both capacity utilization and scale effect are affected by growth.

The effect of scale is well known though difficult to measure precisely. There is, however, a formula that approximates scale effect in the process industries: "Capital cost increases by the six-tenths power of the increase in capacity."

This exponential change is equivalent to an increase of 52 percent in capital cost to provide a 100 percent increase in capacity. The total capital cost became 152 percent instead of 100. The total output became 200 instead of 100. The average became 152/200 = 76 percent of 100 percent. That is a very common and typical experience curve cost decline rate.

Average production unit size normally increases in proportion to rate of total output or even faster. If it does, then capital cost should go down as fast or even faster than in proportion to a 76 percent experience curve. Since capital tends to displace labor over time, then this scale effect becomes increasingly important with growth in volume and experience.

There are limits on scale due to load factors and logistics provided there is a finite total market. But if the total market grows, then scale can be expected to grow too. Scale effect applies to all operations, not just process plants. Marketing, accounting, and all the overhead functions have scale effects also.

Scale effect alone is sufficient to approximate the experience curve effect where growth is constant and scale grows with volume.

For most products, a 70 to 80 percent slope is normal, with the steeper slope for those where the maximum value is added and where shared experience with slower growth areas is least. However, it is probable that few products decline in cost as fast as they could if optimized. It is known that costs are more certain to decline if it is generally expected that they should and will.

It must be remembered that experience curve costs are not accounting conventions. They are cash flow rates divided by output rates. Accounting data is an approximation of this but generally tends to show lower average costs since assets are deferred recognition of cash expenditures. This means that cost of capital and return on capital from value added are both included in experience curve costs. Trading profits or losses from price levels are excluded from this cost calculation.

Experience curve costs on the above basis are probably more accurate representations of cost than any accounting convention, since they are based on cash flow only, not projections, and because such costs include the cost of capital.

The reasons for the experience curve effect are not as important as the fact that the experience curve is a universally observable phenomenon. If costs do not go down in a predictable fashion, then and then only do the underlying reasons become important. Analysis will usually show the reasons to be inadequate investment, improper value added definitions, or occasionally just mismanagement.

Summary

The experience curve is the result of the combined effect of learning, specialization, investment, and scale. The effect of each of these is an approximation and so the experience curve effect itself is also an approximation. The combination of these factors should permit a considerably steeper experience cost curve than is actually observed. However, some additional overhead cost is introduced by the need to coordinate and plan these changes.

All elements of cost do not have the same experience base. Also, some cost elements share experience with other products. Consequently, only new and unique products with completely new cost elements can be expected to go down the cost experience curve with the maximum slope.

4. THE EXPERIENCE CURVE: THE GROWTH SHARE MATRIX, OR THE PRODUCT PORTFOLIO

The use of cash is proportional to the rate of growth of any product. The generation of cash is a function of market share because of the experience curve effect. (See Figure 2−1.)

The growth share matrix is a diagram of the normal relationship of cash use and cash generation. (See Figure 2−2.) *Stars* are in the upper left quadrant. They grow rapidly and therefore use large amounts of cash. However, since they are leaders, they also generate large amounts of cash. Normally, such products are about in balance in net cash flow. Over time all growth slows. Therefore, *stars* eventually become *cash cows* if they hold their market share. If they fail to hold market share, they become *dogs*.

Cash Cows are in the lower left quadrant. Growth is slow, and therefore cash use is low. However, market share is high, and therefore comparative cash generation is also high. *Cash cows* pay the dividends, pay the interest on debt, and cover the corporate overhead.

Dogs are in the lower right quadrant. Both growth and share are low. *Dogs* often report a profit even though they are net cash users. They are essentially worthless. They are cash traps.

Question marks are the real cash traps and the real gambles. They are in the upper right quadrant. Their cash needs are great because of their growth. Yet, their cash generation is very low because their market share is low. Left alone *question marks* are sure losers. They can require years of heavy cash investment. Yet, if they do not develop a leading market position before the growth slows, they become just big *dogs*. Yet *question marks* are very difficult to convert into *stars*. Increase in market share compounds cash needs. The cost of acquiring market share doubly compounds the cash needs. *Question marks* are sometimes big winners if backed to the limit, but most *question marks* are big losers.

The growth share matrix is directly derived from the experience curve. The experience curve is the means of measuring probable competitive cost differentials. A difference in market share of 2 to 1 should produce about 20 percent or more differential in pretax cost on value added. This is equivalent to 5 to 25 percent and more after-tax differential on revenues depending on asset turnover and percentage value added.

The cash flow reference is to the largest competitor in the product. The growth share matrix can be drawn with market share shown in Figure 2−3. Only *one* competitor can be on the left of 1.0. All others are smaller by definition.

Figure 2−1.   Use of Cash Proportional to the Rate of Growth.

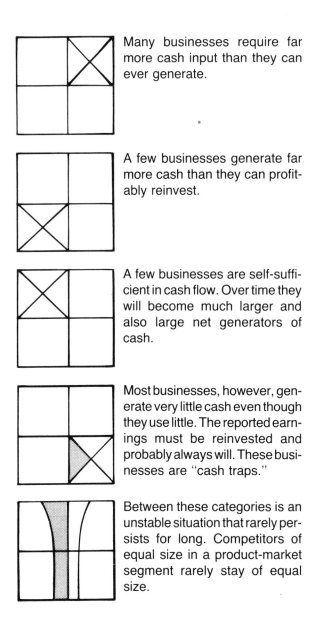

Many businesses require far more cash input than they can ever generate.

A few businesses generate far more cash than they can profitably reinvest.

A few businesses are self-sufficient in cash flow. Over time they will become much larger and also large net generators of cash.

Most businesses, however, generate very little cash even though they use little. The reported earnings must be reinvested and probably always will. These businesses are "cash traps."

Between these categories is an unstable situation that rarely persists for long. Competitors of equal size in a product-market segment rarely stay of equal size.

Figure 2−2.   Cash Generation vs Cash Use.

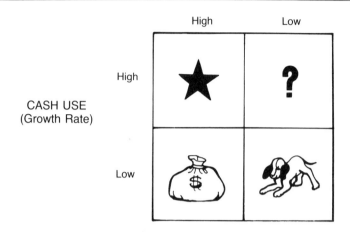

Figure 2−3.   Ratio to Market Share of Largest Competitor.

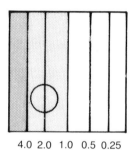

4.0 2.0 1.0 0.5 0.25

Characteristically, a normal experience curve slope will produce cost ratios to the largest competitor like those in Figure 2−4. When the cost differential is less than this, it is usually because of shared experience. Failure to achieve this differential can also be caused by inadequate investment or poor management. Sometimes the segment itself has been improperly identified, and the market share being measured is not the relevant market.

Growth can be shown in terms of the capital opportunity alternatives (Figure 2−5). Growth that is less than the company investment threshold cutoff rate means that the present cash generation is more valuable than the future equivalent. Growth that is more than this means the payoff grows faster than the available alternate investments.

All of the products of a company can be shown on a single growth share

Figure 2-4. Relative Cost Compared to Relative Market Share.

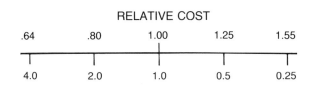

Figure 2-5. Growth in Terms of Capital Opportunity Alternatives.

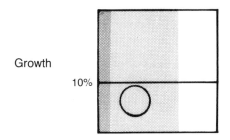

matrix as a product portfolio. Each product can be plotted on its own growth and share coordinates. The size of the product can be indicated by a circle in proportional scale (Figure 2-6). If all products are plotted on a single matrix, then the company's whole portfolio can be shown on a single display (Figure 2-7). This can be combined with a display to show the direction in which each product is moving (Figure 2-8). Nothing should be in the upper sector in which industry growth exceeds your growth. This is death valley. Either manage for net cash flow and get out or gain market share.

Typically most *products* have less market share than the leading competitor. Yet, it is typical also that the weighted average market share of most *companies* exceeds 1.0 on such a display (Figure 2-9). Such a single chart with a projected position five years out is sufficient alone to tell a company's profitability, debt capacity, growth potential, dividend potential, and competitive strength.

Growth share matrices and related charts are valuable tools for analyzing strategic positions and options. Great care must be taken in product-market segmentation before drawing such charts, however. It is quite possible for a company to be the largest in the industry and be a leader in no single segment.

Figure 2−6. Products Shown on a Single Growth-Share Matrix.

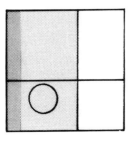

Figure 2−7. A Typical Successful Diversified Company.

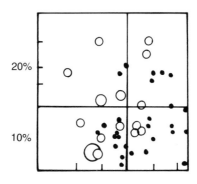

Figure 2−8. Comparative Growth Rates.

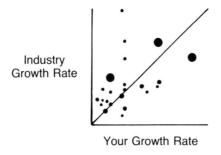

Figure 2–9.   Relative Weighted Average Share versus Largest Competitor.

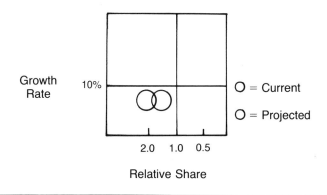

5. THE EXPERIENCE CURVE: PRICE STABILITY

Whenever real (deflated) prices fail to parallel real (deflated) cost trends, then market shares shift. When market share shifts, then relative costs of competitors also shift. The market leader with the largest share will lose share eventually if prices do not go down as fast as his costs.

When prices decline faster than the leader's costs on trend, there is always some competitor who is growing faster than the industry average. That competitor's margin will usually stay constant while all other competitors' margins shrink. Price and market share are stable only when prices are declining in parallel to costs *and* prices are low enough to prevent gain in share by high cost competitors.

Costs characteristically decline 20 to 30 percent in real terms each time accumulated experience doubles. This means that when inflation is factored out costs should always decline. The decline is fast if growth is fast and slow if growth is slow.

It is obvious that prices must approximately parallel costs over time. Otherwise margins would constantly widen on trend, or conversely, they would continually narrow and then become negative. But costs net of inflation do continually decline as a function of experience. This experience curve effect can be observed in all manner of products and services.

Two characteristic patterns can be observed in almost all kinds of prices. In one, the prices parallel costs after removing inflation. Examples are crushed rock and integrated circuits (Figures 2−10 and 2−11) (all charts are loga-rithmic scale on both axes).

In the other pattern, prices remain nearly constant, declining very slowly. Then at some point in time, prices begin to decline much more sharply than in the previous pattern. Examples are gas ranges and polyvinylchloride (Figures 2−12 and 2−13).

Characteristically, the price during the initial flat portion of the curve is a constant price in the "then current" value. But if inflation is removed, the real price declines slowly in "constant" money value.

A constant price is a strategic target. The increasing margin of the leader is an attractive inducement to enter and to grow even faster. Yet any reduction in share of the leader also reduces his rate of accumulation of experience and slows his rate of cost reduction (Figure 2−14). The new entry starts at high costs but reduces those costs rapidly because of the faster rate of growth.

Competitors are racing each other down the cost curve by accumulating experience. If X grows enough faster than Y, the relative costs can be reversed (Figure 2−15). The interaction between the competitors produces a continu-ing shift in their relative margins.

Differences in growth rate determine the potential rate of shift in margin between two competitors. For practical purposes there can only be one price or "price equivalent" at equilibrium between vendors of equivalent products. If any competitor is willing to sell at a lower price, he will tend to gain share and grow faster and thereafter improve his relative margin unless all others match the price change.

Figure 2−10.   Prices Paralleling Costs after Removing Inflation (Crushed and Broken Limestone).

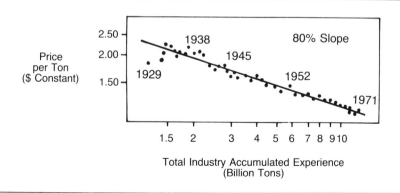

Source: U.S. Bureau of Mines

Figure 2–11. Prices Paralleling Costs after Removing Inflation (Integrated Circuits).

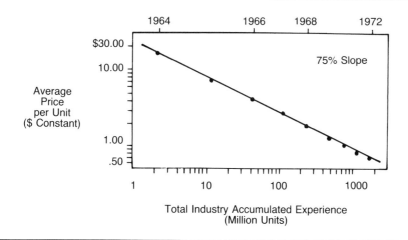

Source: Published Data of Electronics Industry Association

Figure 2–12. Prices Nearly Constant with Sudden Sharp Decline (Freestanding Gas Ranges).

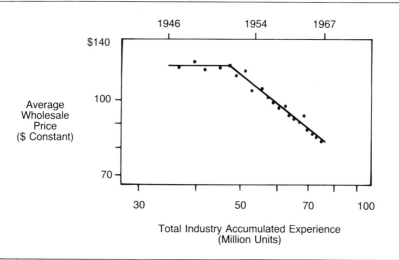

Figure 2−13. Prices Nearly Constant with Sudden Sharp Decline (Polyvinylchloride).

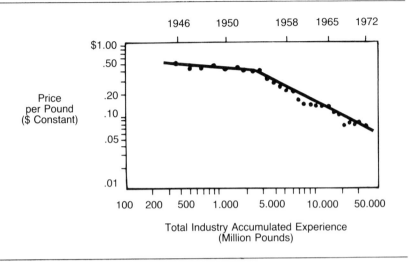

Figure 2−14. Cost Reduction Slowed by Reduction in Share.

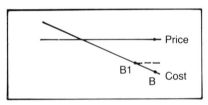

Figure 2−15. Relative Costs Reversed by Accumulation of Experience.

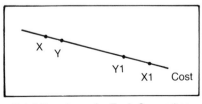

Prices are stable only when three conditions are met:

1. The growth rate for all competitors is approximately the same;
2. Prices are paralleling costs; and
3. Prices of all competitors are roughly equal for equal value.

A change in price will not change price stability except temporarily unless it changes relative growth rate of competitors. Temporary price changes matched by competitors have essentially no effect on relative cost or on stability.

However, a price change that affects competitors' relative growth rate will affect price stability eventually. Paradoxically, long-term effects tend to be the reverse of short-term effects. An increase in price tends to encourage growth in capacity as well as affect financial resources. Rarely will all competitors be affected equally by any price change. If any competitor changes growth rate, prices will be destabilized if *any* competitor tries to maintain previous profit margins. The competitor who loses share will eventually have to charge relatively more and vice versa.

In the United States, a majority of new or fast-growing products go through a two-phase cycle. The first phase has steady prices or very slowly declining prices in constant dollars. This phase is followed by another phase of a long period of steeply declining prices. Usually only one competitor will be able to preserve profit margins. It is always the fastest growing competitor. (See Figure 2−16).

The break in price is characteristically triggered by some combination of:

• a very successful and aggressive new entry willing and able to maintain a modest profit margin;
• growth of new entries at a rate that eventually preempts all growth from the original leader; and
• an economic recession that produces temporary significant overcapacity. (See Figure 2−17).

The fastest-growing competitor has the fastest decrease in costs and as soon as costs are below current price has an option: (1) maintain constant margins and convert decreasing costs into lower prices, or (2) hold prices and let the margin widen. The first option tends to perpetuate the cost decline in addition to perpetuating the high growth rate. The second stabilizes prices but stops shift in cost and market share.

If the fastest-growing competitor maintains a constant margin, it can then lower prices faster than anyone else's costs can decline. The strong probability

Figure 2—16. Two-Phase Pattern of Fast-Growing Products.

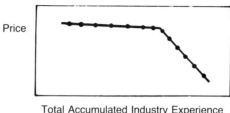

Total Accumulated Industry Experience

Figure 2—17. Pattern of Initial Price Advantage, Rapid Gain in Market Share, and Constant Margin.

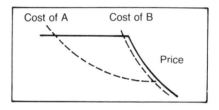

Figure 2—18. Japanese Pattern of Steady Decline in Prices Parallel to Costs.

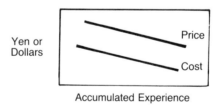

Accumulated Experience

is created that competition with shrinking margins will not invest to maintain margin. Small competitors are often conceded a price differential until they become large and low-cost competitors.

By contrast almost all prices in Japan follow a pattern in which prices steadily decline in parallel to costs (Figure 2—18). Market share tends to be more stable in Japan than in the United States. In Japan the efficient producer tends to grow faster than the higher cost competitor. In the United States the reverse is often true.

Price stability is determined by the willingness of the leader and low-cost competitor to set prices that are low enough to inhibit growth faster than the market by any competitor. Price stability is maintained by the low-cost competitor maintaining prices parallel to his costs. Any other policies will destabilize prices and shift market share.

6. THE APPLICATION AND MISAPPLICATION OF THE EXPERIENCE CURVE

Knowledge of the experience curve and its characteristics is of little value unless it can be used to increase the competitive effectiveness of those who understand it. The experience curve has been both applied and misapplied in the past.

The most obvious application is the prediction of achievable cost levels in the future. Probably the most valuable application is predicting probable future cost differentials between specific competitors. A possible use is the prediction of the probable shift in cost weighting of the components of the unit cost. But any real use of the experience curve has significant risk of error unless its true characteristics and limitations are understood.

Origins of the Experience Curve

The first known formal use of the experience curve in strategy formulation was in 1966 in a presentation of the Boston Consulting Group to the General Instrument Corporation with respect to the probable cost behavior in the future of the then infant MIS technology. The basic principles of the experience curve as then expressed have stood up well, in spite of the fact that the understanding of the experience curve phenomenon itself was then only at an elementary stage.[1]

The validity of the concept itself and its usefulness have been confirmed and reconfirmed. However, the experience curve has been misunderstood and misapplied often enough to cause some loss of confidence in its usefulness.

Only a few years after the experience curve became general knowledge, it was applied as the basis for the horizontal axis of a two-by-two matrix known as the growth/share matrix. The vertical axis was the rate of physical growth in volume of a product. This matrix was only a schematic which was useful in dramatizing a relationship. "Products which grow need more capital. Products which have a competitive advantage generate more capital than those that do not." Market share was used as a surrogate for cost advantage based on the experience curve relationships.

Soon afterwards the research of the Strategic Planning Institute with PIMS by Buzzell and Schoefler demonstrated a very distinct and high correlation between market share and cost.

The now familiar star, cash cow, dog, and question mark quadrant names soon became part of the business vocabulary.

The concept of business portfolio management was given considerable standing and impetus by the use of the growth/share matrix as a schematic.[2]

The Dangers of Misreading the Curve

The qualitative relationships of the experience curve and the growth/share matrix are valid and very important. But the policy implications can be quite misleading.

The customary "bubble charts" or "spot charts" derived from the growth/share matrix exhibit corporate portfolios based on industry market share for various products. They have often been used to analyze corporate portfolio balance. With appropriate analysis they may be useful in focusing attention on cash flow imbalance. However, with appropriate product and market definitions, they may be even more useful to evaluate management performance. Any product that does not move rapidly toward 100 percent of the relevant market share is presumably mismanaged. It is persevering in competing in significant parts of its market where it is at a disadvantage, it is not capitalizing on its advantage, or it does not know its competitive relationships well enough to manage its resources. This assumes that the market is defined as that portion of the competitive arena in which a competitor has a new advantage over all others.

Competitive differences and market shares based upon inappropriate product definitions, inappropriate market definitions, and incomparable experience curves are worse than useless. They are misleading.

What the Risks Are

As a schematic for focusing attention and providing a conceptual framework, both the experience curve and the growth/share matrix can be quite useful. As a basis for policy determination there are serious risks. It is a temptation to overgeneralize without sufficient understanding of the underlying causes and the second-order effects. Analysis can only be a qualitative judgment when definitions are amorphous. For example, the PIMS definition of a market is the "served market." This is a rather indeterminate denominator for a fraction that represents market share. The definition of the products that make up the market is often equally ambiguous. Such products are often only parts of families of products. Frequently such products only partially share their cost elements and their characteristics. Imputing probable cost differences based on share of the market has some risks when neither products nor markets can be defined with any precision.

Using the experience curve as a surrogate for differentials in competitive costs also has some hazards. To do so with confidence you must know competitors' growth rates and relative cost positions by products. Market share has a very uncertain meaning if each competitor has only a portion of the market relevant to his competitors and vice versa. The whole question of market definition becomes quite critical in any quantitative assessment. Products and services are rarely identical between competitors. Typically, they dominate different segments of the same generalized market. Under such conditions, there is little reason for expecting their costs to have more than a partial common basis.

Concept of a Market

The conventional definitions of markets and costs are inherently too ambiguous and too imprecise to be useful in identifying the significance of changing percentage differences in market share.

If any two competitors compete for exactly the same customers with exactly the same products in exactly the same way, then there is no way for either to have a competitive advantage. Even if they could, the relationship would be unstable. Any temporary net advantage could be leveraged into an even greater advantage if the competitors were otherwise identical.

In the absence of a net competitive advantage, there is no likelihood of a profit for any competitor. When competitors do exist and both do have a profit margin in spite of true competition, then it can only be because each has a differential advantage with respect to the other.

The parallel to this in biological competition is known as "Gause's Principle of Mutual Exclusion." The differences between competitors may be subtle and complex and be part of whole systems of differences. Yet it is the comparative advantage of each competitor with respect to any other given competitor that is critical to their mutual coexistence. Those differences must logically be applicable to differences in domain, segment, or market within which each individual has an advantage over the others. Logically, in this context every competitor should dominate that portion of the environment, or market, where it has an advantage. Attempting to compete consistently beyond the boundary of one's own advantage is a sure way to reduce and average down one's competitive advantage.

Relative Advantage

Such relative mutual advantages can exist simultaneously only if the competitors are different from each other. Both must have an advantage with respect to a different portion of the total possible market. That difference may be in a large spectrum of factors which include anything that is relevant to the competitive relationship. If this hypothesis is logical and relevant, then any stable relationship between profitable competitors must be based on significant differences in either customers or products or that situation is unstable. Continued stability requires that any changes in or by any competitor must always leave each competitor with a net advantage. There must be a boundary between their respective advantages. Crossing that boundary by either competitor must create a disadvantage, otherwise the competitive equilibrium is unstable. True competition with stability depends on shifting the "no advantage boundary."

Good management requires dominating 100 percent of the market in which you have an advantage. Failure to do so is failure to compete or failure to manage. Good strategy is management that protects the "no advantage boundary" that now exists while focusing on expanding the boundary against some competitor at some point.

The concept of market as described is not conventional. But conventional concepts of markets and competition leave much to be desired. Rare indeed is the market that has such abrupt boundaries and discontinuities that boundaries can be identified by discrete barriers. The differences between competitors and markets are like the differences between individual people. It is a broad-band spectrum, and the gradations are very important. Categories of products and markets to be used in experience curve analysis are often equally imprecise and amorphous.

The use of industry average experience in experience curve analysis is almost a contradiction in terms. It is probably irrelevant. The experience and behavior of the low-cost competitor are the controls.

The use of an analysis of a growth/share matrix based on industry market shares or industry experience can be no better than a qualitative schematic.

Basing analysis on industry characteristics is like assuming that all family members are alike and make their living in the identical way. Industry characteristics are irrelevant unless the reasons for stable competitor equilibrium in the industry are known with confidence.

The concept of "perfect competition" denies all that we know about competitive behavior. Competitive equilibrium depends upon competitive stability. The individual competitors constrain each other and must be in stable equilibrium with each other. The more alike they are, the more severe their competition will be, and the more unstable their relative position will be. The same is true of categories of competition. Continued survival for any or all depends upon uniqueness of advantage no matter how small the scope of that advantage may be.

The Availability and Use of Data

None of the above implies that the experience curve is not real, or that the experience curve is not very useful in analyzing competitive differences. However, intelligent use of the experience curve requires understanding of its fundamental characteristics. Day and Montgomery pointed out the lack of precision in the supporting evidence on the experience curve. "Unfortunately, the bulk of the evidence in support of the experience curve has been graphical in nature and has not focused on the measurement and economic issues." This is true. It is also inevitable.

Price Data

Price data are almost the only kind of public data that can be found for experience curves. Obviously, prices must be parallel with costs for those who survive and remain competitive over significant periods of time. However, for shorter periods of time there can be major deviations of prices from the trend. These can be caused by cyclical variations. They can be transients caused by the effects of shifts in market leadership or in market share.

They can also be caused by periods of aggressive, nonsustainable competition. Price experience curves can only suggest the trend-line cost changes of that competitor who can and does take the initiative in setting the price level.

Cost Data

Even where detailed internal cost data are available, they must be converted to a different form to be useful in the construction of experience curves. The basic data for experience curves should be accumulated cash expenditures and accumulated physical output. The rate of change in the trend line of that ratio is the rate of decline in unit costs. Conventional cost data are almost always available in forms consistent with generally accepted accounting principles. GAAP treat cash expenditures as assets until they can be applied as cost to the revenue with which they are matched. Yet because of inflation, the eventual revenues are in dollars of different value from the original expenditures. Deflating costs before income tax effects does not recognize the hidden inflation surtax which has been added to taxes. All assets on the balance sheet were bought with dollars of higher value than the dollar revenues with which they are eventually matched.

This depreciation in the value of money is ignored for tax purposes and the difference in cost and revenue due to inflation is taxed exactly as if it were real profit. The only way to recognize this in constructing experience curves is to treat all cash expenditures for taxes as part of the cost of capital. At the same time, all cash flows must be accumulated in constant dollars.

A large proportion of most accounting costs have substantial portions that are allocated and therefore estimated, assumed, or forecasted. These allocated costs, which may have no relationship to changes in cash flow or physical volume, determine the cost for analyzing the experience curve.

The use of conventional accounting costs for constructing experience curves can be misleading. However, this problem can be circumvented. Physical units can be compared with constant dollar cash flow expenditures.

Cash expenditures cannot steadily parallel output if there is any investment for the future. Investments are periodic and precede the revenue they create. Consequently, the ratio of cash flow/physical output is inherently erratic. But, accumulated cash expenditure divided by accumulated output is average cost.

Average cost starts high because initial investment precedes revenue to be derived from that investment. Any return on investment must eventually result in an increment in value of output in excess of the cost of the investment. Consequently, the compounding of capital input will produce constantly declining cost as long as the cost of the capital is also included as part of the investment. In this sense the experience curve's cost decline is inevitable if there is any net return on capital invested and that capital is not withdrawn.

This part of the net return does not depend upon the price as long as the unit revenue exceeds the unit cost. Any further margin between cost and revenue is generation of additional investable capital or profit.

The experience curve is the rate of change in the cumulative cash input divided by the cumulative physical output. The denominator and the numerator are both cumulative. Because of that, the ratio between them is exponentially smoothed. If the experience curve rate of cost decline is constant, then the current unit cost will become the cumulative average cost when the total cumulative experience has doubled.

This relationship between cumulative cash input and cumulative physical output is the central issue of the experience curve. It is the rate of change in that ratio which is the rate of cost decline of unit cost with each doubling of total output.

The experience curve is inherently a trend-line phenomenon. Accounting costs will show a different pattern of costs from experience curve costs. Characteristically, accounting costs will show unit costs which abruptly increase after a major investment. Unit costs will then exhibit a typical decay curve pattern of decline to below the experience curve, only to abruptly increase again with new major investment.

If the product itself and its price could be defined and measured with real precision, then the parallelism between the cost experience curve and price experience curve would be a very significant measure of the stability of competitive behavior. The differences between the two curves would also be an accurate indicator of the return on revenues over and above costs of capital. Unfortunately, this is not likely to be possible.

Definitions and Adaptation

Very few indeed are the products or services that will continue to have the same real relative value over time compared with the average of all other products and services. All progress requires change. All change forces adaptation on those who are part of the changing environment. They in turn are part of the environment of their suppliers and their customers and all others who constitute their network of interactions. This constant adaptation means that product definition, characteristics, and requirements are constantly changing. The same is true of markets and customers.

Plows have gone down a cost experience curve since the days when a crooked stick was pulled by an ox. Now gang plows are pulled by tractors. The price of the plow has gone ever upward even in constant value money. But the cost of plowing an acre has gone steadily down. What is the unit of value produced? And what is the real product? Consider the transport aircraft. In fifty years it has gone from the Ford *trimotor* to the 747 SP and the Concorde. What is the real product? All are airplanes. The Piper Cub and the B-1 Bomber are both airplanes too. What share of the market did they have?

At times, products proliferate into families with common elements but which individually are required to be quite different in order to compete within their particular domain. For such reasons the experience curve of a given product can, and often does, have a shifting definition and shifting array of competitors. Each of those competitors is quite likely to be changing in its capabilities. Each of them may be required to adapt in order to continue coexistence with each other. This is why the long-term trend which is the inherent characteristic of an experience curve can never be really precise. Its units of measure, components, required product characteristics are constantly changing. The most remarkable characteristic of the experience curve is that it is so ubiquitous and so consistent in spite of these variables.

Why There is an Experience Curve

The experience curve has demonstrated that almost every product will go down a reasonably predictable pattern of cost decline, in terms of value added, when expressed in constant value money. This is not surprising if we reflect on the fact that gross national product increases year after year.

We produce more real output per capita year after year. Isn't that the equivalent to a decrease in cost per capita? If we divide gross national product by population and deflate to determine constant dollars, we find that output per capita has increased on trend by several percent per year in most of the developed countries of the world. This is the equivalent of saying that the output per hour of work has been going up steadily and consistently too.

If this happens consistently over a period of centuries, then there must be a characteristic pattern that causes this phenomenon. What are the categories of cost reduction?

First and foremost is the development of better tools. It makes little difference whether we are referring to an electric motor or to a sharper knife. The principle remains the same. Regardless of the eventual value, the creation of any tool means the deferral of consumption and the diversion of time, effort, and energy to the construction of the tool. That is investment. Any investment has four characteristics:

(1)   It requires the investment *before* the benefits can be obtained. That is the equivalent of deferral of the ability to consume immediately.

(2)   The total benefits obtained must exceed the investment made previously and provide additional benefits beyond that. That is the return on the investment.

(3)   Until the original investment is compensated for, there can be no profit, only waste and a loss. The return on investment is a measure of both the amount of the surplus of output over input and the time required to receive those benefits.

(4)   Any investment that provides more total output than the total input is a net increase in output, and therefore an increase in productivity.

The second major factor in productivity is elimination of waste. Waste is any effort, use of time, or use of energy that does not add to the value of the end product. An obvious example is defective work. Less obvious but equally real is the cost of storage including the material handling and the recordkeeping that it entails. Anything that could be omitted or reduced without reducing the output or the net value of the end output is, by definition, a waste. Time spent in nonproductive activities or not utilized is a waste whether or not it is people, time, or machine use.

The third major form of productivity increase is substitution. This includes anything in any form that makes it possible to get better results with less effort. It is an increase in productivity and therefore a decrease in cost.

A fourth major factor is knowledge. Knowledge is the ability to know which things can be done and how. Knowledge too has a cost. Knowledge requires investment to acquire. Knowledge requires time to acquire and time to relate and to apply.

All of these factors have interrelationships. Just as knowledge is investment, so is a tool. So is an elimination of waste; so is the task of substitution. All of these factors interact with each other in a complex set of feedbacks and trade-offs.

Scale, learning, adaptation, and investment are the principal causes of the experience curve effect. Technology is often mentioned as a factor in cost decline. But technology is a derivative of investment, learning, and adaptation. There is little way to predict those things that have never been done. But once it is known that it can be done, then it is a question of time, investment, and learning until it can be duplicated by others.

Growth, like technology, is a derivative. All change reduces or reverses the growth of those things being displaced. Simultaneously it accelerates the growth of those things that are becoming more cost-effective. Rapid growth can become self-reinforcing and vice versa because of the experience curve effect.

Scale may not be a source of cost reduction unless it is required for growth. A cost reduction that is not accompanied by an increase in total output must be paid for by a reduction in operating cost. The cost of the capital involved must be offset by the reduction in operating cost that results. Otherwise there is no cost reduction.

Scale Effects

An increase in scale without an increase in output must displace smaller units which will no longer be needed. An investment on a larger scale under those circumstances requires that the total unit cost of the large-scale unit, including return of capital and cost of capital, must be less than the operating cost alone of the displaced units, after crediting scrap value. Otherwise there is no cost reduction.

When there is sufficient growth to require the added larger-scale unit, then the new unit cost becomes the average of the old unit cost and the newer larger-scale unit.

These calculations become difficult when the operating cost differentials become large and yet there are large seasonal or cyclical variations in demand for output. The newer and larger-scale unit typically has the lowest unit operating cost. But the older and higher operating cost unit may still be more cost-effective for peaks of demand. An increased size of large-scale unit might have its capacity unused except for peaks. The experience curve will eventually reflect the wisdom and foresight of these capacity and cost reduction investments. However, the pricing policies and competitive environment will determine both demand and margin. In any case, the slower the growth the less likely scale is to offer cost declines.

The consumption of electric power in the United States has not only ceased growing, it has declined slightly. The purchase of large-scale power plants has almost disappeared. For the foreseeable future, the only market may be for small peak-load units in spite of the fact that the unit cost of the power they generate is much higher than the cost of large units, provided the large units can operate at a full load continuously. The airlines face similar problems of evaluating the value of scale in cost reduction.

Shifting Cost Components

The cost of any service or product of any complexity is made up of many separate components. Each of these cost components goes down an experience curve of its own. Except in the very newest of technologies, many of the cost components will have long histories. Frequently these past experiences will be shared with other components or other users through common suppliers. The beginnings of these past experiences will often be at different points in time.

As a consequence of these factors, different cost components can have different rates of cost decrease and different rates of change in relative cost levels even though they have the identical amount of experience as common components.

Initially the cost of the electronic watch was dominated by the cost of the semiconductors. That cost declined rapidly as a function of time. The display and power unit did not decline as fast as a function of time. The cost decline of the case and strap was even slower. The cost of marketing declined very little. Yet each of these cost components could be, and probably was, going down its cost experience curve at approximately an equal rate of cost decline. There had been vast amounts of marketing of watches before the electronic watch came along.

In the watch itself there have been substitutions of components because of differential rates of cost decline resulting from differential rates of growth.

Effective application of the experience curve requires the analysis of substitution effects, shared experience, relative growth rates and components, and, most of all, careful definitions of competitive boundaries of comparative advantage.

Experience Elasticity Life Cycle

Progress down the experience curve depends upon product volume growth rate. On the experience curve, a doubling of experience will produce a given amount of cost decline. If there is no growth, then each doubling of experience will take twice as long. Without growth, cost declines steadily slow down until eventually they disappear.

If growth rate of experience is a constant growth rate, then the rate of cost decline will also stay a constant percentage.

There is a feedback loop between price elasticity and growth rate. Any given rate of cost decline on the experience curve requires a corresponding rate of increase in total experience. If that reduction in cost is translated into an equal percentage reduction in price, then the price elasticity should produce an increase in volume. That volume increase may be either more or less than that required to produce the cost decrease. If it is less, then the growth rate of volume and of experience will decrease. If it is more, then the growth rate of volume will increase at a compound rate.

This is the basis of the life cycle of a product. The interaction between the experience curve and the price elasticity curve defines the shape of the volume life cycle. Starting from zero volume, almost any significant growth will be at a high percentage rate. Exponential compound growth requires extremely high price elasticity to be sustained. While elasticity is a very difficult parameter to measure, it should be possible to correlate the shifting growth rate of volume with the changes in the price level and determine the imputed shape of the price elasticity curve. If this can be done with reasonable confidence, then it should be possible to forecast the life cycle of a product with some confidence.

There are two risks in this. The product itself is constantly shifting in character and cost components. The characteristics of competitors are also constantly shifting. For a given competitor, the price elasticity can shift substantially depending upon the evolution of other competitors.

Summary

The experience curve is a valuable conceptual framework for long-range strategy development. It is not suitable for cost control or forecasting over short time spans. For effective application, it requires careful analysis of the definitions of cost components and the definitions of products and markets. It can be misleading when applied to policy decisions if it is used without reference to the effects that will be common to competitors.

All competitors tend to come down some form of experience curve. The critical question is, "Who is coming down in cost the fastest?"

Future research should focus more on a conceptual framework for describing the system effects in business competition. When that has been accomplished, then the experience curve will become a far more useful concept. It is itself an example of a complex system of interactions.

NOTES

1. Boston Consulting Group, "History of the Experience Curve," *Perspective* No. 125 (1973).
2. Day and Montgomery, "Diagnosing the Experience Curve," *Journal of Marketing*, (Spring 1983).

7. COST OF CAPITAL

Misconception about the cost of capital can cripple a company's growth and ability to compete. Decisionmaking must be based on additional cost of added capital versus additional return on that capital. The *net* return differential on added investment is all that really matters.

Most corporate capital in Western business comes from retained earnings. The cost of that capital is the present value of whatever the shareholder eventually receives. If it is a high return, it is also very high cost. The income tax approximately doubles the cost to the company of equity capital.

Debt is always the lowest-cost capital as long as there is a clear and apparent ability to service that debt. If the pretax return on equity ever sinks to the level of the interest rate on debt for any significant time span, then the company is in serious trouble.

The "average cost of capital" is a very seductive, dangerous, and fallacious concept for investment decision. The highest average cost of capital belongs to the no-debt, highly successful firm. If that average cost of capital is used for investment decision, then the more successful the firm, the fewer the opportunities it will have to invest.

By contrast, a marginal, debt-ridden competitor can justify more debt as long as it will earn more than the debt service on the new investment. He can grow and lower his costs while his lower-cost competitor cannot.

This kind of logic causes the most successful and secure firm to deny itself the opportunities and the leverage available to its weaker competitors.

Debt is the lowest-cost source of *additional* capital. It could be used to leverage profits. But it can also be used to sell at lower prices with equal profit to the shareholder or to pay more for resources without reducing return on shareholders' investment.

The capital markets recognize this. The competitor with the highest debt to equity ratio usually enjoys the highest price to earnings ratio if other things are equal. The reason is obvious. A higher debt-to-equity ratio leads to higher growth rates and lower costs if the debt has been used to improve cost and position in already successful businesses.

The true cost of capital can never be separated from its use. The highest-cost and highest-risk capital of all is what is *not* used to improve a competitive differential.

8. DEPRECIATION

Depreciation is based on a fallacy. Depreciation does not affect profit; it affects the forecast of future profit. There is only one profit that counts: That is the cash payout to the owner. Depreciation does not affect cash flow except by changing the income taxes.

Corporate "reported profit" is a paper profit that may never be realized. Probably no company has ever paid out dividends equal to its accumulated "reported profits." Few ever will. Most corporations' complete lifetime dividend payouts are less than half their cumulative lifetime reported earnings. The difference is represented on the asset side of the balance sheet. Every asset except cash is merely a forecast that someday that asset will be converted into cash—maybe.

Meanwhile the "reported profits" not paid out are represented by the assets. These assets, no matter how valued, are the business. They are not retained profit. They are investments in the future that may produce profit—real profit that can be paid out in cash—someday.

It should be obvious that any tax on "reported profit" is a withdrawal of capital. The consequences are far-reaching. If the capital is withdrawn in proportion to success then the inefficient is protected from the efficient. The whole basis and purpose of a competitive economy is undermined by a tax on "reported profit."

Depreciation is the critical issue in determining the tax impact of "reported profits." Depreciation applies to fixed assets where the benefits are long deferred and problematical. Current assets are near cash. Fixed assets are nowhere near a profit.

The sensible thing to do, of course, is to use 100 percent depreciation for tax purposes, i.e. expense with expenditures. This would prevent withdrawal of capital by taxes until capital was no longer invested. The effect would be to defer, but also *increase*, taxes. The other effects would be to increase competition, decrease prices, increase national productivity, and dampen inflation.

— No corporation would consider investing in assets where the return is less than on government bonds. Most set minimum thresholds for investment four or five times as high. Deferred taxes invested in earning assets would increase the present value of future government tax receipts.

— If increased competition passed the benefits of deferred taxes on to consumers in the form of lower prices then the control of inflation would be benefitted.

— If deferred taxes permitted the efficient to grow faster than the inefficient then everyone would benefit.

Obviously the consumer, the government, and the economy would benefit most if taxes were based on dividends only. They are not. The next best thing would be taxes based on a cash resource, cash expenditure basis. They are not. The best available choice under current laws would be the maximum possible depreciation rate, up to 100 percent annually.

Business management has little choice or influence in tax policy. Neither can business determine its own "reported profit." But in making policy decisions there is still a fundamental rule that should be the guide: "Cash is compounded until it becomes cash out" is all that counts. Cash is all that counts. Anything else is a forecast.

9. CASH TRAPS

Most products in most companies are cash traps. They will absorb more money forever than they will generate. This is true even though they may show a profit according to the books of account. Continued investment sends good money after bad. Escape from the trap requires extreme measures. Either stop investing and manage solely to maximize cash withdrawal, or invest so heavily that a leading position is reached in the market.

Reported profit always exceeds payout to owners in any business over time. Much of the reported profit must necessarily be reinvested just to maintain competitive position and finance inflation. If the required reinvestment, including increased working capital, exceeds reported profit plus increase in permanent debt capacity, then it is a cash trap. Cash is rarely ever recovered from a cash trap unless relative competitive performance is improved by obtaining a superior market share.

Historically, the typical manufacturing company with typical growth rates and asset turnover had to have a pretax profit of about 7 percent on sales, or the entire company became a cash trap. Fast-growth sectors of the economy required even higher margins. So did capital-intensive businesses. At any lesser margin, the required increase in assets exceeded the reported profit. This cannot continue, unless the permanent debt also increases in the same proportion, or new equity is constantly added.

With higher rates of inflation, the minimum required return is increased in proportion. Inflation of assets must be financed and will never be recovered in dividends or liquidation.

Real cash traps are worthless because the owners will never receive a payout. Instead, the owners will put in cash. Reported profit is not payout. Even if you escape from such a cash trap eventually, you have still lost. The longer it takes to escape, the greater the loss in present value of your investment.

It is a fact that most net cash generation of virtually all companies comes from a very few products that have a clearly dominant share of their relevant product-market segment. This is inevitable.

Pareto, an Italian economist, discovered this effect many years ago while trying to determine why most of the wealth was concentrated in a few families. It is a familiar pattern: Approximately 20 percent of the items produce approximately 80 percent of the margin. However, when a constant reinvestment requirement is subtracted from all margins, then that 20 percent may well represent 120 percent or more of the actual net cash generation.

Pareto's Law alone would lead to most of the net cash generation coming from only a small number of products. The experience curve effect compounds the relationship and couples cash generation to market share. The experience curve effect causes your relative cost to decrease about 20 to 25 percent each time your market share doubles. Both margin and volume increase with increase in market share. The converse is true also, of course. That is why there are many cash traps, and most of them are low-market-share products.

Reported profit is irrelevant to the shareholder. All he will ever receive is a cash payout of either dividends or liquidation value. This is all a corporation receives internally from a product: either net cash throwoff or net liquidation proceeds. Regardless of reported profit, a business or product is worthless unless it compounds and returns the cash invested in it.

In a dynamic economy almost every business, even slow-growth ones, require reinvestment of a substantial proportion of reported profit. Inflation alone requires financial growth to compensate for inflation in asset values as they turn over. Additional growth in assets employed is required in order to maintain market share as the industry grows with the economy. Consequently, only a portion of the reported profit can ever be available for distribution unless the business is liquidated. If it is liquidated, many assets will prove to be unconvertible into cash at book value.

When profit margins are low, the required reinvestment will often exceed the reported profit indefinitely, even in mature stable businesses. Do nothing and such businesses trap cash forever. The longer the delay until liquidation, the greater the loss. If eventual liquidation will produce only a portion of book value, then the reported profit until then is being overstated in proportion. If the company's required threshold on investment return is higher than this deflated profit, then the difference represents the company's annual opportunity cost.

Fast-growth products are even more dangerous cash traps than slow-growth products. Growth compounds the cash input required. But growth alone does not improve relative cost or profit compared to competition. The eventual payout depends on a superior cost compared to competition whose margin is just sufficient to finance growth needed to maintain their own market share. Superior margin is rarely achieved without superior market share. Consequently, growth just compounds the cash drain unless it also leads to superior market share.

The only advantage of a growth product is that share can be shifted more rapidly from one competitor to another by preempting the share of the growth itself. The disadvantage of a growth product is that it usually requires a large negative cash flow just to hold position in the market. Yet failure to achieve a leading position before the growth slows can be fatal to any hope of a cash payout later.

The critical market share seems to be a level about twice that of the largest competitor. At about that point, debt capacity increases with market share even faster than the assets required. The cost level that can be achieved makes it possible to service debt equal to total net assets employed even though competition is selling at cost or below. When this condition is reached, the entire reported profit and more can be withdrawn as cash and reinvested elsewhere or paid out. It is a highly desirable position. This leads to a competitive rule of thumb: Take at least twice as much of the growth as your leading competitor in any relevant product-market segment; if you cannot, then plan the process of extricating your investment as expeditiously as possible.

Only the largest two or three competitors in any product-market segment can reasonably expect to avoid being a cash trap. There are usually several times that many active competitors. Therefore, the majority of the products in the average company must be cash traps. This means that a majority of the products in the average company are not only worthless but a perpetual drain on corporate resources.

Prices could be lower to customers and profit could be higher at the same time if all competitors would recognize their cash traps and stop wasting money on them. Anytime there are more than two or three active competitors in a given product-market segment, then someone is making a mistake. The leader may be failing to compete by holding an umbrella over higher cost competition at his own expense. Or, it may be that competitors are caught in cash traps. Either way, major opportunities are being lost.

3 PRICING

1. PRICE STRATEGY WITH INFLATION

Experience curve theory says that about 3 percent steady annual growth on trend in physical volume is required to reduce costs enough to offset each 1 percent of annual inflation. Only products with growth rates more than three times inflation can expect to hold a constant price in current dollars without producing a shakeout.

There are some general pricing rules:

Price parallel to experience curve costs if market shares are to be kept constant.

Raise prices faster than experience curve costs to cause the smaller producers to grow fastest.

Lower prices faster than experience curve costs to shakeout all except a few competitors.

These relationships are not affected by inflation. However, inflation has the effect of an automatic price cut if you do not raise dollar prices.

Significant inflation cannot be offset by growth except in a very few fast-growth products. Therefore, constant prices in current dollars mean an automatic competitive shakeout for most products. Even maintaining margins in slow-growth products requires upward price leadership by someone. Failure to raise prices during inflation is, in fact, a price war of attrition.

The effects of price changes are very unequal. Low-share competitors are characteristically high cost. Failure to increase prices is very punishing to them. Failure to increase prices during inflation naturally tends to concentrate market share in the already leading producer.

However, if anyone increases prices and everyone else does not follow, the competitor who holds prices constant will tend to gain share rapidly. Often he will gain share fast enough to offset the lower price. If the price differential is allowed to exist for an extended period the growth in volume will lead eventually to an improvement in relative cost for the competitor gaining share. This can actually more than offset the price decrease on trend if capacity is added fast enough to keep lead time low.

It is ironic that public policy calls for holding prices during inflation. The inevitable result is the squeezing out of the higher-cost and smaller competitors. The same action in the absence of inflation would be viewed as extremely aggressive.

The corporate strategist must first decide whether market share is worth buying before he can evaluate pricing strategy. Inflation does offer the leading producer a chance to methodically lower real prices and slowly squeeze out his higher-cost competition. He can do this by just holding prices constant.

This is no small opportunity. True prices can be steadily reduced this way. In a noninflationary environment, the same result would require a series of highly visible steps that would provoke very strong reaction from competitors and perhaps from antitrust administrators.

Experience curves and inflation work in opposite directions. In the absence of inflation, the leading producer tends to hold prices up in the face of declining costs until his loss of market share becomes unbearable. His very size provides the opportunity to maintain a price umbrella. With inflation every producer is automatically the price leader on the down side until he takes specific action to raise prices.

Passive price behavior by the leading producer means that without inflation he keeps prices too high for his own good in fast growth situations. He loses share steadily and prices eventually decline anyhow.

Passive price behavior by the leading producer in modest and slow-growth industries during inflation means that it steadily lowers the price to below the level of his competitors' costs. No one else can raise prices to offset inflation unless the leading producer will follow.

Inflation changes the direction in which active price decisions must be made. However, inflation does not change the fact that there is an equilibrium price at which market share will stay constant. Either higher or lower levels will cause share to shift. Inflation makes the equilibrium price a moving target with an upward bias.

2. PRICE TACTICS UNDER PROFIT MARGIN CONTROL

A price reduction can be an investment. It can also be a potent competitive weapon. A price reduction now can be worth more than the profit now. So if price controls limit margins, it may be no loss. The best investment is to cut price levels on the least profitable products while increasing capacity on the more profitable ones.

Profit margins should rise rapidly during a recovery from a depression. Costs have been pared to their minimum. Unused capacity exists. A large portion of the cyclical volume increase can flow directly into profit margin. As volume approaches capacity, margins also approach a maximum. If that margin is limited by law, a choice must be made. Either prices must be lowered or expenses must be increased. What is the best investment?

Expense increases are not usually a good investment unless expenses were cut too far previously. Of course increased advertising, increased R&D, increased training are all legitimate expenses. However, the value received may be less than the cost if expense is increased.

The expense portion of a capacity addition is more likely to be rewarding—if more capacity can be used. All capacity increases have noncapitalizable expense that precedes capacity availability. Added capacity in itself reduces profit margin until the added volume absorbs the increased overhead. However, capacity additions rarely make sense, except for the more profitable products or for products where share is being gained rapidly.

The first objective under profit margin control should be to use existing capacity fully. Volume is not limited, only the margin in percentage is controlled. The second objective should be to prevent capacity additions by competitors in your own most profitable products. All price reductions should have one of these two objectives. Some reductions can contribute to both objectives.

A price reduction is the most effective in increasing volume and using capacity when your market share is low. The large competitor's total cost to match a price reduction is higher in direct proportion to his higher market share. Low-share competitors are often conceded a price differential for that reason. Price reductions are most likely to buy you added volume if your market share is low.

Low-share products are typically also low-profit or unprofitable products. However, the absolute profit is immaterial; it is the added margin available on the increased volume that counts. Characteristically, a price reduction equal to approximately half of the unused capacity in percentage points has a good chance of being recovered in volume variance if the market share is low. To this extent, you get a 100 percent return of your investment plus the permitted margin on the added volume. Reduce price, but stop reinvestment. This is important. These products are cash traps if you expand capacity. They were unprofitable before you reduced price. They can only be profitable at capacity.

If the high-share competitor who has previously been holding market share should match the price reduction of a competitor who has a low share, he will accomplish little immediately except to resolve his own profit margin problems in a most painful way.

High-share products are typically both important in size and highly profitable. Prices must have been kept at least low enough in the past to inhibit competitive growth because the critical element in market share shift long-term is almost always capacity availability. The only reason for lowering price in such a product is to discourage capacity investment by competitors. Your own capacity additions properly publicized can be a substantial inhibitor.

If you are the largest share competitor, you should be the most profitable. If you are the most profitable, you should be able to afford to have more capacity available at peak periods than your competitors. If your competitors also have ample capacity at peak periods, your prices are probably too high. The low-share competitors are probably gaining share. In that case, reduce your prices now while you still have your margin and your market share. Forget controls, and worry about competition.

Market share shifts most often due to differences in lead times or availability. This is a direct function of capacity. The effect is sharpest at the peaks in business activity. If you are the most profitable, you should add capacity first. Our economy is still growing. Capacity will be added by someone.

If current profit margins are limited by controls, then the expense of capacity addition temporarily reduces margin while at the same time your visible expansion tends to discourage competitive expansion.

Inflation will surely continue, even if at a reduced rate. Constant price levels are therefore effectively price reductions except in the fast growth areas. Increased capacity by the market leader while holding constant prices will squeeze out the competition in most industries.

The basic tactics under margin control should be therefore:

— Reduce prices on low-share, low-profit items, but stop all investment in added capacity.
— Hold prices on high-share, high-profit items, but reduce current margin by incurring the expenses needed for capacity expansion.

Everyone who does will make a higher profit when price controls end, or even if they do not.

3. SHORTAGES

Do you want shortages? Then put controls on profits. Any restraint on profits in a competitive economy will rapidly produce shortages. If you do not have effective competition, then that is a different kind of problem and requires a different kind of solution.

Every productive enterprise requires assets. Those assets must grow in proportion to the growth of the enterprise. (See Table 3—1.) That takes money. The money supply must be based upon profit. No one will knowingly lend money to a company that does not have the prospects of earning an adequate profit to service the debt. Credit is based upon profit. If you want growth, then profits are a prerequisite.

Financial growth is essential to offset inflation even in a stagnant economy. Real growth in output always requires more capital. Shut off the profit and you shut off the growth in capital. In financial terms the U.S. economy has grown at better than 5 percent in almost every year good and bad for twenty years. Growth is impossible without profit unless there is a rich uncle who will continually lend money to a nonprofitable enterprise.

There is a formula known as the "sustainable growth formula." It relates return on assets, debt, dividends, and growth. No company can sustain growth that exceeds the growth in the shareholder's equity.

This relationship is easily observable over time or in any steady state situation—for example, the aggregate of Fortune 500. Compare the growth rate in the GNP. Try it on the aggregate of the companies represented in the first section of the Tokyo stock exchange, and then compare the calculated growth with the actual growth of the Japanese GNP. Compare the calculated sustainable growth rate of General Motors, Ford, and Chrysler with the actual

Table 3–1.   The Growth Formula.

A firm's rate of growth is equal to its return on equity if no dividends are paid. We can define the return (profit) as the rate of return less interest on the debt. Symbolically, this is

$$\text{Profit} = r(TA) - iD,$$

where   r   = rate of return
TA = total assets
i   = interest rate
D   = debt
E   = equity.

Since total assets are equal to the sum of debt and equity, we may rewrite the expression as

$$\text{Profit} = r(D + E) - iD$$

or

$$\text{Profit} = rD + rE - iD.$$

If the whole expression is divided through by E (equity), it becomes

$$\frac{\text{Profit}}{\text{Equity}} = r\frac{D}{E} + r\frac{E}{E} - i\frac{D}{E}\;.$$

This can be rewritten as

$$\frac{\text{Profit}}{\text{Equity}} = \frac{D}{E}(r - i) + r$$

or

$$\text{growth rate} = \frac{D}{E}(r - i) + r.$$

Since dividend payments reduce this rate of growth, the effect of dividends may be introduced by multiplying the expression by p, the percentage of earnings *retained*. The growth formula thus becomes

$$\mathbf{g = \frac{D}{E}(r - i)p + rp,}$$

where g   = rate of growth
D = debt
E   = equity
r   = rate of return
i   = interest rate
p   = percentage of earnings retained.

Source: *Growth and Financial Strategies,* The Boston Consulting Group, 1968, 1971.

growth in revenues of each company. Try it on General Electric, or DuPont, or any major company. You might find it interesting to check out your favorite growth stock.

Tell your senator and your congressman: "Restrict dividends all that you wish to. That would stimulate both investment and growth. But don't restrict profits if you want growth. Controls on profits are a prescription for increasing unemployment."

4. ANATOMY OF THE CASH COW

The first objective of corporate strategy is protection of the cash generators. In almost every company a few products and market sectors are the principal source of net cash generated. These are the cash cows.

The cash cows fund their own growth. They pay the corporate dividend. They pay the corporate overhead. They pay the corporate interest charges. They supply the funds for R&D. They supply the investment resource for other products. They justify the debt capacity for the whole company. Protect them.

By definition a cash cow has a return on assets that exceeds the growth rate. Only if that is true will it generate more cash than it uses.

This requires high return and slow growth if the cash generation is to be high. Almost invariably the cash cow has a high market share relative to the next two or three competitors. The experience curve relationships would predict that. (See Figure 3—1.)

The debt capacity of the cash cow standing alone is always high. The net cash generation provides high interest coverage and debt repayment assurance.

Figure 3—1.   The Cash Cow's High Return.

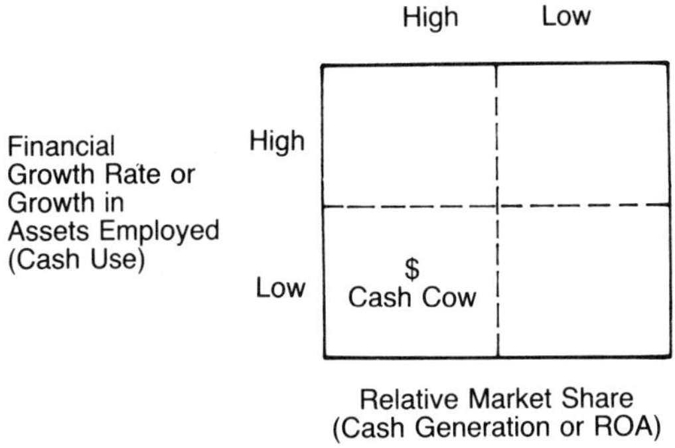

Increased market share for the cash cow frequently increases the debt capacity much more than it increases the total assets employed. This makes possible a leveraging of shareholder investment that can be converted either into higher return on net assets or into lower prices in order to buy more market share. Or the leverage can be converted into increased cash generated for use of other businesses.

There is a limit to the market share of the cash cow. The total cost of buying market share gets greater and greater as the share increases since the margin on total volume is affected. The total value of market share available becomes less and less as the remaining share becomes small. When market share exceeds twice the next largest competitor and four times the second largest competitor, there is rarely any incentive to gain more.

Conversely, market share of a cash cow can be sold off for a very high price in near-term cash flow. A price umbrella converts all the higher price into cash flow and profit multiplied by total volume. However, the competition can increase their growth under a price shelter. The result is a continuing loss of both volume and relative cost potential for the cash cow. Eventually the growing capability of competitors removes the value of the remaining market share until the cash cow goes dry.

The value of the cash cow's market share is almost always higher than the value of any competitor's market share, point for point. This is because the higher market share can and should produce a lower cost than competitors' on equivalent investment.

If it is properly leveraged to equate risk with higher-cost competitors, the cash cow can be a very high generator of cash and profit on the net investment. Yet the decision to invest or disinvest in a cash cow's market share depends upon the alternate opportunities for investment in other parts of the corporate portfolio.

The real value of a cash cow is the discounted present value of the projected cash generated. A high discount rate will almost invariably favor liquidation because of the emphasis on near-term cash flow. The reported profit and net cash flow tend to be parallel and near equal in a low-growth business. Consequently, many cash cows are unwillingly liquidated by short-time horizon profit budgets even though there is no alternate investment that would yield the same net return on net assets.

The real test of value of a cash cow is the net return on net investment when the cash cow has been leveraged with debt to the point at which its break-even cost as a percentage of revenue is the same as the break-even cost of the largest share alternate competitor. To be valid, this comparison must be made after the competitor has also been leveraged to his optimum debt usage.

This test will frequently show that both competitors have high potential returns on net investment. But if extended to each successively smaller competitor, it will eventually reach the one whose net return is no greater than the GNP growth including inflation. It is then possible to determine the true return for each competitor. Rarely will more than three or four competitors be involved if the market is both stable and competitive.

The marginal competitor whose net cash flow just finances the investment required to maintain his market position is worthless except in liquidation. Yet such a competitor is the ultimate reference. All competitors with superior costs and margins can convert that margin differential into a net cash throwoff. That is how to determine the output of a cash cow: The value of a cash cow is determined by the rate of return on alternate corporate portfolio investments that must be used as the basic discount rate on the cash cow's output.

Do you wish to buy or sell market share for your cash cow? If you buy share, where will the money come from? If you sell, where will the money be reinvested that you receive?

4 DEBT

1. STRATEGIC USE OF DEBT

Debt, properly used, can be a potent weapon in corporate strategy. The company who can safely use the most debt can pay more for its assets, sell for lower prices, or grow faster than its competitors. It can do all of this without sacrifice of any profitability to its stockholders.

The concept known as "pool of funds" says that one dollar is like another and therefore it is rate of return on assets alone that counts. But it seems obvious that the stockholder's only interest is the rate of return on equity. It seems equally obvious that return on assets means little until the relative risks have been equated. Investment in some assets carries more risk than others. Some investments because of their lack of risk can justify more leverage than others. Loading one or the other investment with debt is a means of equating risks.

Evaluation of risk in actuarial or quantitative terms is rarely practiced in any complex business. However, risks can be made equivalent for many conditions merely by recognizing the different kinds of leverage and compensating for them.

There are three kinds of leverage: financial leverage, fixed cost leverage, and marginal utility leverage. Debt is financial leverage. The investment can be less and the return per dollar of investment proportionally more. So can the losses. Debt increases sensitivity to price and volume.

Fixed charges produce the same kind of leverage. The higher the fixed charges, the higher the sensitivity to changes in price or volume.

Marginal utility has the exact same effect. The investment is lower and the percentage return is usually higher. But the sensitivity to price or volume change is proportionally great. For example, the marginal mine is cheap to buy but is uneconomic except when prices are high.

All three kinds of risk with respect to price and volume can be equated by the use of debt as a compensating factor in calculating rate of return. Perhaps it is the lingering memory of the liquidity crisis of the 1930s, but debt still carries a degree of apprehension not similarly attached to new ventures, high investment in plant, or to the many other forms of business exposure of equal impact. It is clear, however, that the risks of debt should be evaluated on the same basis as other kinds of business risk. Failure to equate these kinds of risks and to balance the one against the other leads to an inadequate use of debt and a failure to realize the maximum growth potential inherent in corporate resources.

Different kinds of investment can be balanced in terms of risk by considering the lower-risk project to be loaded with enough debt to make its fixed charges equivalent to those of the higher-risk investment. The result is often surprising: The net return on equity for the safe investment can easily be higher than on the high-return investment after the risks are balanced. Nowhere is this more clear than in the case of the banking industry with its high effective debt-to-equity ratios. After-tax rates of return available to banks are low, by business standards, yet many businessmen would be happy to earn comparable returns on shareholders' investment or enjoy similar rates of earnings growth. The same is true of insurance companies, whose debt to equity ratio is in the hundreds.

The firm that fully utilizes its debt capacity has the inherent advantage of being able to accept lower rates of return on total investment but with equivalent return on equity. This can enable a favorably situated competitor to pay a high price for a resource and still achieve a given rate of return with an acceptable risk. Conversely, the competitor with the highest unused debt capability has to sell its product at the lowest profit margin and still be otherwise completely equal in performance. Failure to understand this equation, with a consequent over-appraisal of the risks of debt, may result in a firm's being priced out of the market.

It is important to realize that competitive superiority can be converted into either higher return on equity or lower risk under extreme conditions. In turn this relationship can be converted into either lower prices or higher return for the same risk. Where competitive position is price sensitive, debt can become a major strategic weapon.

The efficient company with the higher profit margins and the greater earnings' stability can justify the highest debt/equity ratio. It can, therefore, support the highest return on shareholders' equity and, in turn, the highest sustainable rate of growth.

Paradoxically, failure to use debt properly is often a major strategic error committed by the *strongest* firms. The prevailing view is that whatever the benefits of leverage for firms at a marked competitive disadvantage, market leaders, with greater capital resources at their disposal, enhance strength by avoiding debt. However, underutilization of debt by the leader can allow less favored competitors to grow faster, set lower prices, and show higher rates of return on stockholder equity. The proper use of debt sometimes allows the high-cost firm to grow faster and reach efficient size, while the market leader appears helpless to duplicate the performance.

Explicit determination of corporate risk, and its equivalent in terms of an optimum debt/equity ratio, is a matter of strategic importance. The strategic use of financial power is no less crucial, nor any different, from the utilization of operating strengths. For capital-intensive industries in particular, it may well be the most critical factor in strategy.

2. THE DEBT PARADOX

The companies who should use debt do not. Their higher cost competitors often steadily displace them by the effective use of debt. It is a paradox that the unwillingness of low-cost companies to take financial risks by the use of debt exposes them to far greater competitive risks. The low-cost competitor would eventually displace any other competitor if he used the same debt and dividend policies.

It is obvious that gearing or leverage can be converted into lower prices at equal profits instead of higher profits at equal prices. It is also obvious that the most profitable firm must grow the fastest if it retains the same proportion of its profits. Consequently, equal financial policies will push prices down until the higher-cost producer stops growing as fast as the low-cost producer. Eventually, the high-cost competitor will not find it worthwhile to reinvest even depreciation, and he will be displaced.

This is the sequence that should be expected in a competitive economy. It rarely happens, of course. The reluctance to compete fully can be caused by:

— cartels that maintain prices or antitrust constraints;
— belief that profits now are preferable to market share;
— fear of government censure of an increasing concentration of market share or corporate size;
— misperception of the relative risk of debt versus risk from competitors; and
— faulty management objectives such as "return on assets."

All of these reasons are dubious and difficult to defend:

— Cartels cannot maintain prices unless they can also police share of production. If prices are fixed, competition merely shifts from price to services that are the equivalent in added cost to a price reduction. The only real control on prices is almost always the willingness to add investment by a competitor.
— Profit now can be worth more than a higher share later. But the high-cost producer should always be inhibited first on that line of reasoning.
— Fear of antitrust is a valid constraint in the United States where the objective is fragmentation for social purposes regardless of economics. But the same thing happens in the United Kingdom where the constraint is nearly invisible.
— Debt has risk attached, particularly in a deep recession or a liquidity crisis. But the risk is always greater for the high-cost competitor. Risk of loss in market share is usually even greater. Shifts in market share result in shifts in relative cost because of the "experience curve effect."
— Many firms attach great importance to "return on assets," yet it is return on shareholder's investment that affects the shareholder.

Debt is a potent competitive weapon. It is a paradox that it is almost always used by those who are in the poorest position to use it safely. Those who can use debt with telling effect are the very ones who avoid its use. The low-cost company can increase the return to shareholders, increase its own growth rate, and reduce prices, while reducing the competitive risk. Everyone loses as a result of the debt paradox: the consumer, the shareholder and the economy. The only winner is the high-cost competitor who survives and grows while being spared by his more efficient competitors:

— Lower cost means wider profit margins.

— Wider profit margins mean more debt capacity with equal safety.

— More debt means either faster growth or lower prices at the same return to the shareholder.

— Either faster growth or lower prices displace the high-cost competitor.

— Failure to use debt fully is a failure to compete.

— Failure to compete is a breakdown of the free enterprise system and an invitation to government regulation as a substitute for competition.

The whole free enterprise system concept is questionable in its basic validity unless low-cost competitors are willing to use equal debt and retain earnings equal to their less efficient competitors until they displace them.

3. MORE DEBT OR NONE?

Use more debt than your competition or get out of the business. Any other policy is either self-limiting, no-win, or a bet that the competition will go bankrupt before they displace you.

If you are the low-cost competitor, you can carry more debt with less risk than your competition. That debt could be converted into more profit by leverage. But it can also be converted into lower prices at the same profit, while both decreasing the risk from competitors and maintaining a lower overall risk level than competition.

Failure of the low-cost competitor to use more debt than its competition is self-limiting. It is failure to compete. It is also a failure to maximize share-holder profits at risk levels below the competition's risk.

A high-cost competitor must use more debt to survive and grow unless more efficient or fortunate competitors unwittingly hold a price umbrella. A higher permanent debt level is the only way for the high-cost competitor to compensate for higher costs while still maintaining competitive prices and growth rates.

Without higher debt, the high-cost competitor is in a no-win position. The higher-cost competitor must lose market share if it maintains the same debt/equity ratio and uses the same dividend payout ratio as its lower-cost competition. It is inevitable. Relative growth must inevitably be in propor- tion to return on equity under these conditions.

The varying product margins of multiproduct companies often obscure these basic relationships. Failure to focus on the specific financial policies of specific lead competitors and react accordingly compounds the lost opportunity.

Properly used, debt can increase debt capacity faster than it increases the assets in which the debt is invested. Properly used, debt can decrease risk, decrease price, and increase shareholder profit simultaneously.

Proper use of debt will usually require that each product support more debt than any competitor chooses to use. Failure to do so on average is either self-defeating restraint on competition or a no-win position justifying no further investment.

Proper use of debt will inevitably mean that the low-cost competitor drives out all competition, unless antitrust laws force prices to be held up to protect higher cost competition. Few companies minimize their risk by using debt properly.

4. DEBT, SAFETY, AND GROWTH

Superior growth increases debt capacity faster than it increases assets. Each 1 percent difference in competitive growth rate should eventually result in a 0.3 to 0.5 percent cost differential on all costs. This the experience curve effect.

The favorable cost differential would be equivalent to approximately 30 to 50 percent of the differential in revenues. If this is multiplied by the ratio of revenue to net assets, then the rate of return on the added assets can be determined. This is the interest rate that could be paid without affecting the net differential in profit margin compared to the slower-growing competitor.

The ratio between this interest rate and the actual interest rate represents the ratio between increase in debt capacity that can be serviced and additional net assets actually required. If this ratio is larger than one, then debt capacity is actually *increased* by borrowing to increase capacity.

Debt capacity is increased faster than assets by growing faster than competition in the same market segment. Usable debt capacity shrinks if competition grows at a superior rate.

Superior growth rate has its costs. Competition does not concede market share without a struggle. That struggle often means depressed margins for both competitors. Loss in market share means loss of current profit and future

The above examples are based on the experience curve effect (i.e. deflated costs decline 20 to 30 percent each time accumulated experience doubles). Experience and market share tend to be roughly equivalent. The experience curve is an observable fact in most businesses if product and market segments are properly defined and properly managed.

profit margin too. But the cost of new market share is a real investment, just as if it were bricks and mortar.

Gain in market share has a current cost but a future payoff. It is an investment in lower future costs. The difference in cost can be capitalized at the opportunity rate. If 10 percent opportunity cost is reasonable, then 6 to 10 percent of a year's revenues can be sacrificed to gain 1 percent of your own market share (assuming sales/assets $= 2/1$). A higher debt-to-equity ratio can be translated into a higher return on shareholders' equity.

A higher return on shareholders' equity can be translated into higher growth instead. Higher growth can be translated into greater profit margins and, therefore, greater safety at the same debt-to-equity ratio.

Every competitor should use more debt than the competition or withdraw. The high-cost competitor has no other way of offsetting cost disadvantage while achieving superior growth that will permit it to eventually overcome the cost handicap. The low-cost competitor can improve safety while withdrawing capital if it uses superior cost to support higher debt levels. Proper use of debt makes all business competition unstable.

5. THE ANNUAL BUDGET

No process in business is more fateful than the decisions that establish the annual budget. Few decisions are more subjective and less subject to logic and analysis. Any improvement in precision would be a major contribution to business effectiveness. The critical element missing in budget making is the frame of reference. What is an optimum level of budgeted expenditure? And how is it determined?

There are two traditional approaches to budgets: One takes the previous year and demands slightly better net results; the other chooses the desired end result and tailors the budget to fit. Both approaches are essentially the same: compromises between past performance and hope.

The obvious defect in these approaches lies in the highly uncertain realism of either past performance or future hopes as a standard of reference. Under rapidly changing circumstances this evaluation becomes little better than a crude guess. The process becomes a struggle to satisfy the boss, not an effort to optimize performance.

The facts of business life and organization behavior usually force even the most objective and candid supervisor into a game of deception. This takes the form of overstating budgetary needs and forcing the initiative in reducing budgets to start at the top. The middle manager is caught between the ambitions and expectations of subordinates and the conflicting ones of supervisors.

Few organizations have not at some time imposed an overall cut in budget. Almost always this affects the efficient and inefficient alike. An operation that is already optimal is degraded while the inflated operation is merely trimmed. After one such experience, few managers will fail to anticipate the possibility of such a broadly applied budget cut.

The nature of leadership and supervision over a complex organization makes the individual manager the spokesman for his or her group's demands on the earning resources. If the manager fails to advocate the group's aspirations eloquently, acceptability as their leader is weakened. There is no reasonable way for the manager of a subordinate part of the organization to resist the group's demands except by reference to restraints clearly imposed by the central management. How does the central management distinguish between too much, enough, and too little?

A well-run business is a very fine balance between a large number of related activities. Too much or too little of anything can be damaging to competitive performance. Many of these expenses—like research, advertising, and sales effort—are directly subject to management choice.

Under stable competitive conditions, the optimum combination is often approximated by trial and error. In the absence of competition or some equal restraint, these costs tend to multiply indefinitely in accord with the well-known Parkinson's Law. But under competition each competitor can use others as its reference.

When the competitive environment or market shares are changing, it is possible to make gross errors in budget standards with the short-term consequences. The truly difficult part of budget setting is that a large part of the benefits and other consequences of a given expenditure level are delayed in time. The problem would be relatively simple if all cause and effect were immediate. Because this is not the case, many business opportunities are dependent on actions that appear dysfunctional short-term.

In fact, budgets are set by feel and by guess rather than logic, except when there are specific constraints imposed by competition on strategy. The ultimate logic must be based on cost-versus-value analysis. This in turn depends on a factual appraisal of benefits. Benefits can be evaluated only with respect to investment returns.

All expenditures are investments even though some have very quick return and some take years. Operating budgets are characteristically treated as short-term investments with immediate payout within the accounting period. Obviously, this is rarely true. They are treated this way because of the considerable difficulty in coupling cost and revenue when benefits are indirect.

Difficult as it may seem, it is not an impossible task. For this approach to be feasible, however, budgets must start from a strategy with a specific plan of competitive action translated into sequence and timing of commitment of resources. With a strategy base the overall budget becomes an investment analysis. Cost effectiveness becomes meaningful. Budgets set without a strategy base become mere exhortations to try harder. Budgets based on strategy demand far more than cost control. They also specify what the money buys, and when. Therefore they can be investment analyzed.

6. THE APPROPRIATION REQUEST

Most, perhaps all, companies have a procedure whereby major capital expenditures are individually approved by the board of directors. Traditionally, these are screened on the basis of rate of return. Characteristically, this apparent rate of return is misleading and dysfunctional.

Clearly, there must be some basis for deciding whether to make a new major investment, but apparent rate of return, payback period, or yield is not an adequate index of reliability of return.

Most companies intuitively recognize this, at least in part. It is common to see approval of "safe" investments, such as for storage tanks to permit carload purchase, even though the return is only 12 percent. At the same time, a 40 percent return on a new machine may be refused instinctively because of doubt about the validity of the apparent return. The highly subjective nature of many of these choices indicates the inexactness of the investment standards.

The desire for quantitative investment standards often leads to a wholly nonfunctional and illusory threshold minimum rate of return. "We must have a minimum rate of X percent on all of our capital appropriations." This rarely means much—for at least five separate reasons.

First, the evaluation of risk must be factored explicitly. The rate of return is never a net return until it has been adjusted for sensitivity to price, volume, inflation, and time exposure. For example, the maximum return on assets in the corporate finance company can never be more than a fraction of the required return on a new factory. The return on equity in the finance company can nevertheless be satisfactory indeed. Rate of return means little, even on a comparative basis, until equity has been geared with enough debt to equate price and volume sensitivity on alternate choices.

Second, the project return is immaterial if it is a expenditure necessary to maintain the business as a whole. The classic example, of course, is the rate of return on replacing the flood-damaged bridge on the main line of the railroad. The key variable is always the overall long-term rate of return on the business as a whole. If that is good enough, then you must do what is needed to support it.

Third, projects cannot be evaluated realistically as separate investments without evaluation of the long-term cash throwoff potential of the continuing stream. After all, cash-in versus cash-out is all that really counts. In a healthy growing business area, however, a large part of the returns must inevitably be reinvested to hold position. If those returns are low and stay low, there may never be a cash payoff. Almost no investment in a going business will pay out in cash at a rate as high as the payouts on the individual projects would seem to indicate.

Fourth, there is no good reason for setting a minimum rate of return. Why not invest all the funds available so long as it is the best investment opportunity available and on balance is profitable? A minimum return, net of risk evaluation, is a contradiction in logic: It says no return is better than a small return.

Fifth, inflation is still very much a factor in investment. The effect of inflation can be positive or negative. Investment in a forest can be favorably affected where expenses over time are returned after inflation of the value of the tree. By contrast, a major cash output at the beginning, such as investment in a factory, is adversely affected by inflation.

Experienced businessmen can often intuitively approximate the net effect of these factors. Their feel for value and consequences has been reinforced over time. Yet the trade-offs are too complex to be approximated with precision, particularly when the opportunity is unusual.

Clearly, no single or simple figure such as rate of return can possibly be an adequate index unless all of the underlying assumptions are made quite explicit and then factored to equate them with some corporate norm. For most companies, the appropriation request is more ritual than the analysis.

The alternatives are not obvious. But two facts stand out. One is that the opportunities and return of the business itself must be viewed as the actual net return on any added investment. Second, any investment is a good one if it causes the net compound rate of return on the equity to increase.

This kind of evaluation is by no means simple or straightforward, nor do most corporations have mechanisms for making this evaluation explicit to the board of directors. Although there is a real question whether most companies have an adequate control over the deployment of their financial resources, redeployment of financial resources is the cornerstone of all business strategy.

7. NEW EQUITY ISSUES

Issuing additional new equity by a corporation is equivalent to announcing that management feels the market value of that equity is a gross overvaluation of future prospects. The only alternate explanations are either financial desperation or superficial financial advice.

The income tax is responsible for this. A corporation must earn nearly twice as much pretax to pay a given dividend as it would to pay the same amount in interest. Therefore, it must earn twice as much on equity as it does on the same capital raised as debt. The company shareholders pay *at least* twice as much for new equity as they do for debt.

The real cost of added equity to the company is equal to the present value of all future dividends. That present value must at least equal the equity issue price. The discount rate that equates the two is the equity shareholders' return.

If that new equity return is significantly above the interest cost of borrowed capital, then the present shareholders are being penalized accordingly. This would be true even if there were no income taxes. Since income taxes do exist, this new equity return must be *half* the interest rate on borrowed capital to equate the company cost. That is obviously no bargain for the buyer of the new equity.

If true equity return on the new equity is significantly above interest cost, then the previous shareholders are paying more than twice as much for new capital as the cost of interest. Yet equity return should be substantially higher than debt. The equity owner commits his capital to perpetuity. He also commits himself to involuntarily reinvest a substantial but unknown portion of the equity earnings. The equity holder must get a higher return to justify the immobilization of his capital. Consequently, the company must pay far more after taxes for a dubious difference in corporate capital structure.

The use of debt introduces sinking fund requirements and increased exposure to a liquidity crisis. Efforts to minimize interest may introduce onerous and costly restrictions on financial mobility. However, it is inconceivable that a sound company cannot provide itself liquidity and financial freedom for a cost less than twice normal interest rates.

An excessively large long-term debt issue subordinated to all other debt and without indenture restrictions would hardly carry double the normal interest cost for a company with any credit at all. If the excess funds were invested in short-term governments, the net interest cost would still be far less than the

The British government has recently changed its tax structure to sharply reduce the double taxation of corporate earnings at both the company and the shareholder level. However, the basic principle of establishing an optimum debt-to-equity ratio still remains valid.

cost of equity financing. The short-term governments would provide all the liquidity needed for anything short of a catastrophe.

Equity capital is attractive to management: It is permanently available; it requires no management of cash-flow timing. But it is by far the most costly of all capital. It is the source of capital of last resort. For the desperate company, equity may be the only source of capital. For the extremely risky, high-growth company engaged in winner-take-all competition, it may offer the maximum total capital. For the grossly overvalued company, it may permit cashing in on overvaluation at the expense of the "greater fool." Equity is the source of capital for the marginal company, the new company, the high-risk company, and the overvalued company. Equity is extremely costly, however, to shareholders of the successful, stable company that is a leader in a well-developed industry.

There is an optimum debt-to-equity ratio for every enterprise. It is rarely less than the principal competitor's debt-to-equity ratio if there is real competition; it is usually much higher for the low-cost market leader. If the debt-to-equity ratio is less than this optimum, then the competitive risk is usually greater than the financial risk of more debt. Below-optimum debt is prima facia evidence of failure to compete as well as suboptimization of performance.

Until the optimum debt-to-equity ratio has been achieved, then a new issue of equity is either a mistake, a distress signal, or a public admission that the share price is a gross overevaluation. It often appears that few companies have carefully evaluated the optimum debt-to-equity ratio for their particular competitive environment. By this omission they fall far short of their optimum performance for their shareholders.

8. THE STOCKHOLDER

One organization is the beneficial owner of better than 80 percent of all U.S. profitmaking organizations: the U.S. government.

The U.S. government receives in cash four times as much as the shareholders do in a normal year. Inflation increases the U.S. government's proportionate share; any acceleration of growth increases the government's share.

The net effect of the U.S. tax structure is contra growth. If a company grows, the government withdraws capital while the other shareholders reduce their income to supply capital.

The arithmetic is interesting. A company "reports" a profit of $1.00. It therefore becomes liable for a tax on "reported" earnings of approximately

$0.50. The normal growth of the average company requires that at least half the remaining $0.50 be retained for capital. Therefore, the shareholder receives a dividend of $0.25.

However, the typical shareholder must pay taxes in the 40 percent bracket on the dividend. The government takes $0.40 \times \$0.25 = \$0.10$, leaving the shareholder $\$0.25 - \$0.10 = \$0.15$.

The government has received $0.50 plus $0.10 = $0.60. The shareholder has received $0.15. The ratio is $60/15 = 4:1$. This ratio will stay constant into the indefinite future as long as inflation and growth stay constant. The government gets $\frac{4}{4+1} = 80$ percent of the total cash paid out as profit.

Any increase in growth will require more retained earnings to finance the growth. Unless profit margins go up, this must mean a reduction of dividends, assuming a constant debt-to-equity ratio. So growth in the economy means that the government gets an increased proportion.

The government withdraws capital if a company grows, while the shareholder must reduce his income to replace the capital withdrawn by taxes. Obviously a corporate income tax is designed to inhibit growth.

Inflation is forced financial growth. The net effect of inflation is to reduce shareholder income and increase government income if profit margins are held constant. Yet prices must go up by an amount equal to inflation *plus* the increase in tax to leave the shareholder unharmed. Either prices must go up *more* than inflation, or the government has automatically increased its proportionate share of the cash payment.

The consequences of such tax treatment are far-reaching:

— If an efficient competitor were displaced by an efficient one, the U.S. government would receive 80 percent of the cost differential in taxes.

— Increases in prices by business are highly deflationary. The increase in price is the equivalent of an 80 percent sales tax on the increase.

— In terms of business strategy, the government provides 50 percent of the capital for new investment if that investment is expensed instead of capitalized. It will take 80 percent of the benefits in any case.

— In terms of its own policy, the government would do well for itself to tax dividends instead of reporting earnings. Since the government takes 80 percent of the proceeds, it will *increase* its tax take if the company earns pretax only 1.25 times the U.S. bond rate on the deferred taxes. If the cost reduction is passed on to the customer as lower prices, the government can still recover the added value through its ability to tax the increase in national productivity.

If the U.S. government is unable to rationalize its tax policies, then the financing of growth by debt is a far more attractive and significant strategy. The benefits can be far-reaching, as the Japanese have demonstrated.

9. DIVIDENDS

It is a paradox that dividends are simultaneously the ultimate goal of corporate performance and the signal that significant growth cannot be expected in the future. Growth companies rarely pay more than token dividends. They need their earnings to finance their growth. Mature companies pay a high percentage of dividends because they lack opportunities to invest internally.

It is commonly expected in the United States that a company will pay out 40 to 60 percent of earnings in dividends. This implies the balance is all that can profitably be invested in the business. Payment of a dividend is a tacit admission that the company does not believe it has investment opportunities that are any better than those available to the stockholder. Most stockholders would prefer bigger dividends later to smaller ones now.

The individual who receives a dividend suffers several handicaps in trying to match the corporation's performance. He or she has to compound the dividend with less capital, since the tax paid does not remain part of working capital. If the shareholder receives a dividend the government *immediately* takes part of it in taxes. If the corporation retains the money and reinvests it for the shareholder, payment of a tax is delayed. Consequently, the corporation need not earn as high a return as the shareholder in order eventually to provide the shareholder with the same net gain.

In addition, the company has some tax benefits not shared by the individual. A company can treat some of its investments as expenses. Such investments, including research and advertising, reduce current taxes in proportion to the tax rate. If the investment pays off, the tax collector claims a portion of the return equal to the capital supplied by the tax deferral. If the investment does not pay off, the tax collector shares in the disappointment. The corporation is in a much better position to maximize return than the private investor.

Dividends have a profoundly depressing effect on growth, far greater than

Public policy note: Corporate taxes should be levied on dividends, not reported earnings. Corporations are not consumers; they are investors. There is no profit to a shareholder until it is paid out in dividends. Taxes on reported earnings are in fact a withdrawal of invested capital. Dividends are the only true profit and taxes should reflect this. The tax collector would receive more in the long run, even when computed in terms of present value. As long as the corporation can earn more before taxes on its assets than the interest rates on government bonds, the government tax collector gains by deferring the tax levy until the dividend is paid.

the apparent effect. They are a withdrawal of capital and therefore cut the compounding effect of retained earnings. Even worse, they establish a fixed level of expectation having all of the implied risk and obligation of any fixed charge in an uncertain business climate.

It is not always obvious, but even in a stable, mature industry merely maintaining position requires that a substantial portion of reported earnings be reinvested. This part of earnings can never be paid out as dividends. If all earnings were paid out, the resulting lack of growth would steadily liquidate the company's competitive capability.

Even the balance of earnings after essential reinvestment is not all available for dividends. Inflation takes its share by increasing the cash drain due to taxes. Under inflationary conditions depreciation is never sufficient to cover replacement cost: The difference must be made up from after-tax profit, on which income tax more than equal in amount has been paid. Whenever any asset is replaced at a higher price the change in value of the asset must in effect be treated as a profit. And as such it is taxed. Hence every dollar by which inflation has increased the value of replaceable assets requires that more than 50 cents in cash be used for taxes. The "earnings" reported because of inflation will never be available for dividends.

Only after deducting earnings retained to maintain market share and to offset inflation is there any residue available for competitively superior growth. Even in very profitable slow-growing companies this residue is often not much more than 50 percent of reported earnings. When an equivalent amount is instead being paid out in dividends, company growth cannot for long exceed industry growth.

The use of debt can enable a company to grow faster than its retained earnings are growing—for a while. But dividends not only reduce retained earnings; they reduce debt capacity too. Once a company has reached the optimum debt-to-equity ratio, every dollar of dividends represents the loss of a proportionate amount of debt capacity.

Characteristically, dividends come to be regarded as almost a fixed charge. A reduced dividend is often treated as a distress signal. As a consequence, funds available for debt service are really the residue after dividends. This residue fluctuates; it will not support nearly as much debt as a constant amount would. Therefore dividends in fact often reduce debt capacity far more than in proportion to the optimum debt capacity ratio.

Debt-capacity reduction due to dividends is a serious matter. Debt can be used as a major competitive weapon that permits cutting costs while simultaneously reducing prices, increasing earnings per share, and accelerating growth rate.

A corporation does its stockholder no favor by paying a dividend unless the stockholder has better investment opportunities than the company. Yet dividends are all the stockholder will ever get. The market price of a share merely reflects the present appraisal of the future payout. A sale is merely the transfer of the claim on future dividends. Changes in market prices are merely changes in the forecast of the value of the future payments.

No equity is really worth any more than the present value of its future cash payouts. This present value is dependent on the discount rate applied to its deferred cash payout. Dividends ought to be paid when the present value of the corporation's net future payment on added investment is less than the stockholder himself could get on his investment.

Every corporation that succeeds must pay dividends eventually. The size of the current dividend is a measure of past success. Yet dividends are also evidence of the lack of current investment opportunities.

The policy implication for corporations seems clear. They must retain and reinvest cash that would otherwise be dividends and incur a proportionate amount of debt if they wish to grow as fast as possible. The payment of dividends cuts growth potential even more than the percentage of earnings paid out.

Dividend policy also tells the investor a great deal. A dividend, beyond a token, says the company has not fully used its assets and opportunities; or it says the company cannot be expected to grow any faster than its after-tax equivalent of the interest rate—that is, slowly. The only exceptions are government-regulated monopolies, for which prices, returns, and investments are restricted to a level barely sufficient to finance the desired services. Growth potential and current dividends do not go together.

Index

ABOUT THE AUTHOR

Bruce D. Henderson is Professor of Management at the Owen Graduate School of Management at Vanderbilt University. He is also founder and Chairman of the Board of the Boston Consulting Group, Inc., an international consulting firm specializing in corporate strategy with offices in Boston, Chicago, New York, San Francisco, Los Angeles, Munich, Dusseldorf, London, Paris and Tokyo. Prior to organizing the Boston Consulting Group, he was Senior Vice President of Arthur D. Little and held several vice presidential positions at Westinghouse where he served on the Westinghouse Corporate Management Committee. Bruce Henderson was educated at Vanderbilt University and Harvard Business School.